Translating Literature:
The German Tradition

APPROACHES TO TRANSLATION STUDIES
edited by James S. Holmes

André Lefevere

translating literature: the german tradition

from luther to rosenzweig

Van Gorcum, Assen/Amsterdam, the Netherlands 1977

© 1977 Van Gorcum & Comp. B.V.,P.O. Box 43, Assen, the Netherlands

ISBN 90 232 1513 3

Printed in the Netherlands by Van Gorcum, Assen

Contents

Contents

We Germans have been translating for a long time, and the desire to translate appears to be a national characteristic, since there is hardly a German writer of importance who has not translated, and who does not take as much pride in his translations as he does in his original works . . .

NOVALIS

Preface

Traditions do not "arise". They are consciously shaped and established by a number of people who share the same, or at least analogous, goals over a number of years, decades, or even centuries. They follow a certain pattern: each tradition has its precursors, often "appointed *ex post* by members of the tradition" (Radnitzky, 9). In the tradition shaped in Germany by people sharing a common interest in the translation of literature, the precursors are Martin Luther and Justus Georg Schottel.

Precursors are succeeded by "pioneers — they are polemically oriented on other intellectual traditions flourishing in the intellectual milieu. They formulate the raw program of the tradition and often they formulate its manifesto . . ." (Radnitzky, 9). In the tradition we are concerned with here, this role is filled by Gottsched, who was "polemically oriented on" the French neo-classical ideal as it had lived on into the eighteenth century; by Bodmer, Breitinger, and Lessing, who opposed their own ideal, influenced by Milton and Shakespeare, Addison and Pope, to his; and by Herder, whose polemical orientation on the German past and the concept of history profoundly affected the tradition as a whole.

The pioneers give way to the "masters — they carry out part of the program and their work sets the standard by means of which the disciples measure their success" (Radnitzky, 9). Their contributions to the theory of literary translation are at the centre of this collection. They are, moreover, to a great extent still central to the theory of literary translation as such, whether that theory is formulated in German or not: "Schleiermacher's investigations into hermeneutics and Humboldt's interpretation of understanding are the basis of the whole modern theory of translation, even though this is very seldom so clearly stated" (Huyssen, 52).

Finally, there are the disciples: Wilamowitz, Benjamin, Borchardt, Rosenzweig, and many German theorists of literary translation writing today. It is eloquent proof of the strength of the tradition that the criticism of the disciples has, as far as I know, been limited to internal criticism only. No one writing in German has, to the present day, seriously proposed abandoning the tradition and replacing it with a new one. None of the disciples have, in other words, become external critics who "from a platform outside the tradition attack the very program of the tradition and the adequacy criteria assumed by it" (Radnitzky, 9-10) and become the precursors or the pioneers of a new tradition.

It is important to be aware of the tradition *qua* tradition. Positions taken by certain theorists become fully intelligible only when read in comparison with (or contrasted with) statements made by their predecessors. Thus Schleiermacher's well-known maxim that the translator should either leave the reader in peace and move the author towards him, or *vice versa*, appears first in Bodmer and then in Goethe, whereas Benjamin's essay "The Task of the Translator", much glorified in an Anglo-Saxon world ignorant of the ramifications of the German tradition in translating literature, turns out to be an elaboration on certain thoughts to be found in Herder, Goethe, Schleiermacher, and Schopenhauer.

This collection attempts to outline the development of the tradition of translating literature in Germany. It concentrates on the masters and the pioneers. Less space is allotted to the precursors and the disciples.

The collection by no means contains every single pronouncement ever made by every single German author on the theory of literary translation. It is limited to those statements which have, in my opinion, been influential in shaping the tradition. I have also tried to avoid an abundance of statements by different authors intent on belabouring the same point.

Many early statements, not to mention many statements made by the masters themselves, were never intended to be systematic discussions of all the problems that might arise. On the contrary, most statements deal with the theory of literary translation and with some other topic at the same time. Luther's famous "Circular Letter", for instance, tries to answer two questions: why he translated a certain line from St Paul the way he did, and whether the deceased saints pray for us or not. Similarly, Humboldt's introduction to his translation of Aeschylus'*Agamemnon* contains not only observations on the translation of literature but also an analysis of the *Agamemnon* itself and a highly technical discussion on metrics. I have, therefore, excerpted in many texts what is relevant to the shaping of the tradition, and left the rest untranslated.

Many texts are liberally sprinkled with examples. These have, as a rule, been omitted in this collection, because translations into English of two passages translated into German from Latin and Greek and selected for comparison would hardly serve to make the point the author wanted to make in the original. They would on the other hand spawn a most unwieldy apparatus of notes, comments, and laborious explanations, which could not be farther removed from the theory of literary translation as such.

Most collections of this kind are concerned with historical truth only, that is to say, with "what I establish, on the basis of the most adequate possible hermeneutic interpretation of a text – past or present – as what the historical author said or meant, without taking into account whether I personally think it is true or not" (Seiffert, II, 163). This collection tries to enlist historical truth in the service of systematic truth, that is to say, of "what I, as a human being thinking here and now, must consider true to the best of my knowledge and conscience, on the basis of my present consciousness" (Seiffert, II, 163). In the first case I try to translate, to the best of my abilities, only what Schottel, for instance, or Novalis had to say. In the second case I try to point out what is still valid in their statements and where they have made proposals which are now no longer tenable and will therefore be of little use in the ever unfolding formulation of systematic truth.

These remarks will be found in short commentaries preceding the statements made by the authors translated here. They will take the place of the potted biographies usually found there. They are not intended as summaries; rather, they draw the reader's attention to points made by one author and developed, changed, or contradicted by others.

At the end of each statement there is a bibliographical indication of the source from which the translation was made. As a number of the texts are included in whole or in part in Hans Joachim Störig's collection *Das Problem des Übersetzens* (Darmstadt: Wissenschaftliche Buchgesellchaft, 1963), cross references to that work are given whenever relevant.

What is mine of this book I dedicate to the general editor of the series, who suggested the book and who edited away a number of errors of fact and weaknesses of formulation. The errors and weaknesses that remain are, of course, my own responsibility.

ANDRÉ LEFEVERE

Part One: Establishing the Tradition

Martin Luther, 1483-1546

Luther's *Sendbrief vom Dolmetschen* (Circular Letter on Translating, 1530) is obviously first and foremost a part of the struggles of the Reformation, not a scholarly discussion of translation. Hence the rambling, hortatory, somewhat disjointed style. Hence also the rather summary and unapologetically unscholarly method of argumentation: "I want it this way, I order it this way, let my will be the reason" (taken from Juvenal's *Satires*, 6, 223).

The "Circular Letter" touches on the perennial ills that the translator is heir to: he is badly paid, his work can easily be stolen from him (by a certain Hieronymus Emser in Luther's case) and passed off as someone else's, and he is beset by ignorant and irrelevant criticism.

Luther also sounds the theme of the German nation and the German language. Like many authors after him he uses *übersetzen* (to translate) and *verdeutschen* (to make into German, to "germanize") almost indiscriminately. German language and literature were engaged, in Luther's time and for centuries to come, in fierce competition with foreign languages and literatures: Greek, Latin, French, and, to a much lesser extent, Dutch and English. Part of the translator's task was therefore so to improve German language and literature that they would not be inferior to the competition. This desire to improve leads to a first contradiction, which remains central in the tradition for a long time. "If they [the translators] wanted to cultivate good German, then one of the meanings of 'good' was the pure, colloquial, 'German' German. Yet at the same time they were at work on the German still to be perfected, still to be shaped. If one wanted to shape this German through translation, among other means, without importing any un-German elements one had declared war on, there was a way out: one could give foreign shapes to German raw linguistic material, or one could revive old German words which seemed to correspond to the foreign example . . ." (Senger, 14). Luther, Schottel, Gottsched, Lessing, and Breitinger took the second course. The first found its earliest advocates in Bodmer and Herder.

The translator also has to make the original accessible to those who are unable to gain access to it in its own language, and yet he must, especially if he is translating the words of God Himself, change as little as possible. Hence the second central contradiction: "the Bible translator has two fundamentally opposed duties: the inspired text as *verbum Dei* requires the most exact possible rendering a man is able to provide, so that not an iota of the text is lost. This requirement made by the original is opposed by the requirement that concerns the reader of the translation: the missionary task of the spreading and interpreting of the Word of God. It requires adaptation to the reader's understanding ..." (Senger, 14-15).

Finally, Luther is not engaged in idle boasting when he says that he has "taught both his ungrateful disciples and his enemies to speak". The quality of his translation, his personal stature, and the fact that his dialect occupied a middle position between Low German in the North and the standard being developed at the Habsburg court in the South, all decisively contributed to the shaping of a unified written language for all parts of Europe in which German dialects were spoken.

ENLIGHTEN AND "GERMANIZE"

There has been much talk about the translation of the New Testament and half of the Old. The enemies of truth pretend that the text has been changed or even falsified in many places; therefore many simple Christians, including the learned who do not know Hebrew and Greek, have been overcome by fear and horror. Let us hope that this [the *Sendbrief*] will serve, in part at least, to prevent the abuse of the ungodly and to relieve the scruples of the pious; and perhaps it will even lead to this: that more will be written on this question or matter.

It is clear for all to see that they [the Catholics] are learning how to speak and write German from my translation and my German; they are taking my language away from me, and they knew little about it before. Yet they do not thank me for this, rather they use it against me. But I do not begrudge them because I take pleasure in the fact that I have taught both my ungrateful disciples and my enemies to speak.

We are aware of the scribbler in Dresden who stole my New Testament (I shall not mention his name in my books any more, especially not since he has gone to meet his maker and is well known anyway): he admitted that my German is sweet and good and he realized that he could not do better and yet he wanted to discredit it, so he went and took my New Testament, as I wrote it, almost word for word, and he took my preface, glosses, and name away, wrote his name, preface, and glosses in their stead, and is now selling my New Testament under his name. Oh, dear children, how hurt was I when his prince, in a terrible preface, forbade the reading of Luther's New Testament but also ordered the scribbler's New Testament read, which is exactly the same as the one Luther wrote.

Doctor Martinus Luther wants it this way and says: a papist and an ass are one and the same. Sic volo, sic iubeo, sit pro ratione voluntas.

It is true: those four letters s-o-l-a are not in the original text and those asses' heads stare at them as cows stare at a new gate. But they don't see that those letters correspond to the sense of the text, and if you want to germanize it clearly and forcefully they belong in the translation, for once I had decided to speak German in my translation I wanted to speak real German, not Latin or Greek.

You should not ask the Latin letters how you should speak German, as those asses do, but the mother in the house, the children on the streets, the common man in the market-place, and look into his mouth so that you can learn the way he speaks and translate accordingly: then they will understand and realize that you are speaking German to them.

And if I had taken the best possible German I would have germanized the [angel's] greeting as follows: "God sends you greetings, dear Mary", for that is what the angel wants to say and that is the way he would have spoken if he had wanted to greet her in German.

Whoever wants to translate must have a great supply of words, so that he can call on them immediately, if a word doesn't seem to want to sound right.

I have not taken a penny for it, nor have I looked for one, nor have I gained one.

And yet I have, on the other hand, not dismissed the letter too freely, but I and my helpers have observed it very carefully.

[From Martin Luther, *Sendbrief vom Dolmetschen* (1530), as reprinted in ML, *Sendbrief vom Dolmetschen* (ed. Karl Bischoff; Tübingen: Niemeyer, 2. Aufl., 1965). There are various translations of the *Sendbrief* into English.]

THREE RULES

When we were translating the Bible I laid down the following rules for those who helped me: First: the Holy Scriptures speak of divine words and objects. Second: if a proverb or an expression fits in with the New Testament, use it. Third: pay attention to grammar.

[From Martin Luther, *Summarien über die Psalmen und Ursachen des Dolmetschens* (1532), as reprinted in ML, *Werke* (Kritische Gesamtausgabe; Weimar: Böhlaus, 1883 ff.), XXXVIII,9-69.]

Justus Georg Schottel, 1612-1676

Schottel emphasizes translation's role in improving German language and literature. Language should be improved from within only: no foreign words, locutions, or constructions should actually be imported. Importing foreign knowledge and foreign skills will, on the other hand, enrich the German nation as a whole. The first contradiction appears to be solved, the second is not mentioned.

The extracts given here, from Schottel's essay "Wie man recht verteutschen soll" ('How to Germanize Properly', 1663), were originally written in the form of a dialogue between Siegerath and Wolrahm.

THE TRANSLATOR'S KNOWLEDGE OF HIS MOTHER TONGUE

Siegerath: To know a language and to produce works of art in it that will be conducive to improving the language and stimulating imitation is not the work of a speaker or writer who does not know or learn more than what daily use more or less puts at his disposal. There have been, and still are, many people who, as Germans, can speak and understand German and make so bold as to translate books written in Latin, French, Italian, Spanish, or other languages into German. Such foreign books have, as a rule, been diligently put together in their own language, and the words and locutions proper to that language can be found in them. When a German translator finds these phrases and locutions (they are euphonious in nature and pleasant and quite clear, following common usage and the ways of the land) in the book he wants to translate and his vulgar common knowledge of German does not enable him to find good German phrases equivalent in meaning, he keeps to the German he knows and substitutes German words for foreign words, one after the other, and puts them one behind the other, and should they be expected to have a German meaning and be euphonious in the German language? Rather German words have been made foreign in this miserable manner and the good foreign sense has been germanized, that is, corrupted and disfigured by artificial German. Whoever wants to transfer and germanize must have a good and thorough knowledge of the language he is trying to translate from, and he must also have ready for use a large stock of German words, as Lutherus says — and he must have made such progress in the German language that he is able to recognize its roots and its potential and that he can liberally take from it the good German locutions his translation requires.

THE TRANSLATOR'S DUTY TO IMPROVE HIS MOTHER TONGUE

Siegerath: I have told you this much that you may see with your own eyes that every phrase or locution must sound different in Latin and in German and that words which have been translated one after the other do not mean anything and that it is in the nature of things that they do not keep the sense they had in one language in another.

Wolrahm: I understand now that common knowledge and everyday speech are not sufficient for the production of a really good translation.

Siegerath: Certainly not if, for one thing, the translation has to be good and true, that is, if the true contents of the foreign language that is translated are to be made clear to German understanding by means of true German words and locutions belonging to the German language. And certainly not if, for another, the German language is to be improved by a book translated or germanized; to achieve this the arts, the sciences, history, and other *realia* should be dressed and become known in truly natural German, so that our language, which is rich in words already, will also become rich in artistry and will not smell of un-German Spanish pride, or Italian splendour gone stale, of French pronunciation and circumlocutions that are neither here nor there, or of other things, but it will have its own short and euphonious German nature, rich in meaning and sense.

Wolrahm: But is it not enough to translate and germanize in such a way that the reader can understand the meaning of the foreign language in German words, no matter how they look or sound?

Siegerath: If one understands well the meaning and the contents of the language one wants to translate from and if the words that express this understanding are good German, the *interpretatio* or germanization is good and should not be criticized.

Siegerath: Lutherus, a true master of the German language and a great orator (which praise even his adversaries cannot deny him), has made the German Bible speak true German, so that we do not find any particular aftertaste of Hebrew, Greek, or Latin ways in it. On the contrary: we are well advised to study Lutherus' German version closely and we shall do so to our advantage, as did those who closely studied Cicero's style, or Virgil's, in Rome. We can also learn the art of germanizing from him, and we can look on his way of translating as a signpost and a yardstick.

Siegerath: To stammer German and German words after a foreign fashion is not German and will not become German, and the German language is badly served by such Germanesque. If you want to translate well you must know the language you are going to translate into as well as the foreign language you want to translate from. And when you translate in such a way that the witty inventions of strangers and foreigners are germanized in a clear and intelligible way as far as the nature and capacities of the German language will allow, you will have served the German language well and it will, owing to the noble foreign inventions, take another step towards wealth, health, and perfection.

[Both extracts from Justus Georg Schottel, "Wie man recht verteutschen soll" (1663), as printed in JGS, *Ausführliche Arbeit von der teutschen Haubtsprache* (1663; modern reprint Tübingen: Niemeyer, 1967).]

Johann Christoph Gottsched, 1700-1766

Gottsched extends the idea of "improvement". Translation of models will now be used to improve the skills of individual writers as well as language and literature as a whole. "Translation, as a special form of imitation, achieves its specific importance through the predominance of the idea of a model. It is important for the era of the Enlightenment that not every foreign work, arbitrarily chosen, represents a 'model' in the sense sketched above . . ." (Huber, 4). Only works conforming to the French neo-classical ideal do so. The evil leaders who pervert budding writers are those who oppose that ideal.

Gottsched emphasizes the rendering of sense rather than form. In this he is a faithful adherent to Leibniz' theory of language: words are signs, or even counters. They are freely convertible by means of what almost amounts to a mathematical operation. Equivalents can be found, imports are unnecessary.

Gottsched also sounds the by-now-familiar theme of linguistic nationalism in his condemnation of those who love other languages more than their own. Yet he is not a victim of the "native-speaker syndrome" that was to become so popular with the Romantics and remain so well into the twentieth century. On the contrary he assumes as a matter of course that it is possible to translate not only from a foreign language into one's own, but also from one foreign language into another. He rejects the practice on ethical, not linguistic grounds.

Finally, Gottsched recognizes the value of comparative criticism of translations. This point remains valid today, as does also his point about the use of translation to improve a writer's skill. In teaching, translation turns out to be the most productive method of textual criticism.

Gottsched did not produce a systematic treatise on translation. This was done for him by one of his disciples, Georg Venzky, who in his essay "Das Bild eines geschickten Übersetzers" (The Image of a Proper Translator, 1734) merely repeats and explicitates what Gottsched had written before him. "Not the contents, but the method of Venzky's treatise allow us to speak of [1734 as] the year in which German translation theory was born . . ." (Senger, 10). Unfortunately the method can be seen at work in essays written after Venzky, whereas the concepts can be found in essays written before him. His treatise, which is extremely verbose and pedantic Zto the point of stipulating how much ink the printer should use and speculating about what help the translator may reasonably expect from the Holy Ghost), has therefore not been included in this collection.

CONTEXT AND ADAPTATION TO PERIOD STYLE

Yet I did not imagine that it [making his translation of Horace's *Ars Poetica*, which forms the introduction to his *Critische Dichtkunst*] would be as difficult as I later came to realize. The emphatic syntax of the Latin language, Horace's way of expressing himself, which is sometimes elliptic, and the many artificial words, not to mention the words relating to objects and situations of his time, which are so difficult to put into German — all this, I say, made the work so hard for me that I almost abandoned it after I had translated one-third of it. But a year later I started again and finally succeeded in putting the poem in the state in which I herewith present it to the light of day.

I would not boast to have rendered it line for line, much less word for word: both are in part unnecessary, in part impossible for reasons mentioned above. I have seen myself under the obligation of making seven hundred German lines out of five hundred lines in Latin, even though I never lost sight of the rule that a translator should not become a paraphrast or an explicator. Since I did not omit or change anything of major importance, it is to be hoped that readers will not check too closely whether a complete reproduction of all of Horace's letters and syllables has been achieved. A translator of prose should be checked more closely in this, but a translator of poetry should be allowed a little leeway because of the restrictions he is writing under, as long as he makes up for this shortcoming by writing a pleasant and easy-flowing style.

This has been one of the most important goals I set myself in translating this poem. I very much wanted to translate Horace in such a way that he could be read in our language without irritation and, if possible, with pleasure. I would not have attained that goal if I had not had my doubts about closing my eyes to the correct usage of German syntax and to the purity of metre and rhyme. Our compatriots have a very sweet ear in this respect . . .

This sweetness sometimes goes to such excesses that it is prepared to proclaim the most miserable of rhymes, with all their stupidity and baseness of thought, "beautiful" as long as they exhibit some semblance of natural flow. On the other hand the most beautiful poems of great masters are proclaimed "wretched" and "thin" if there happens to be a little roughness in their diction. Yet since I do not want to agree with those who look for beauty in rough diction, but always call out to them in Horace's words, "Non satis est, pulchra esse poemata; dulcia sunto!" [it is not enough that poems should be beautiful; they should be sweet as well], I cannot, in consequence, reject the taste of those who would rather read a poem with a pleasant flow than a poem that seems forced. Did I therefore not have good cause to be wary of the aversion of sweet ears, especially in a poem in which they should learn to judge the inner beauty of true poetry?

If I have succeeded in this to the extent that I desired, I have no doubt that my work will have its use. It is not in everyone's power to become so acquainted with the Latin of the old poets that they can understand their Horace without difficulty, let alone read him with pleasure. He will therefore be easier to understand in German for many and he will show the right way even to beginners who would perhaps otherwise have allowed themselves to be perverted by evil leaders. There is no doubt that this has already happened to many, but I could prove by my own example, if it were important enough, that many have been brought back to the right path and turned away from the wrong road they were following. The brief notes I have put under the text will not be without their use, I hazard, and they will shed good light on many things. Time-bound objects and situations cannot all be explained in verse in such a way that one can understand them well enough if one is almost two thousand years removed from the author's time. More learned readers, who have no need for them, can leave them unread as they please, the way one usually proceeds with the Latin annotations to older writers when one is well trained in them already. I shall have fully reached my goal if beginners only learn to understand my poet a little better.

[From Johann Christoph Gottsched, *Versuch einer critischen Dichtkunst* (1751), in the modern reprint (Darmstadt: Wissenschaftliche Buchgesellschaft, 1962).]

TRANSLATION AS A MODEL: RULES

[Translation] is precisely what the copying of a given model is to a beginner in the art of painting. We know that the works of great masters are copied with pleasure and diligence by mediocre artists or by beginners who would like to make their way. While they copy the design and the nuances, and paint in full, they observe with the greatest acumen every detail of the art and skill of the original artist, all the beauty and perfection of their example. They also make up a hundred small rules for themselves while they are at work; they commit to memory a hundred technical tricks and advantages which are not immediately known to all and which they would not have hit upon by themselves. Indeed, even their hand acquires a certain skill to guide the brush with more confidence. The same holds true for a translator. When he has a good text in front of him and he wants to translate it into his mother tongue, he pays much greater attention to all the words, expressions, sentences, and articulations of the whole than an ordinary reader would. He notices all the ornaments and the beauty of a passage which others would have overlooked. He steals the art away from the original, so to speak, and acquires, unnoticed, the skill and ability to think and express his thoughts in the same way as his predecessor.

If it is so useful and advisable to translate, the first question to be asked should be when you ought to start training yourself in this way. My reply is: as soon as you understand a foreign language in which there are books of quality available so well that you acquire the confidence to translate it into German.

Another question is what to translate. I want to state in advance that you should not translate from your mother tongue into a foreign language, and neither should you translate from one foreign language into another. This is a task fit only for those who love a foreign or dead language more than they love their own, and would rather be at home with other nations than with their own people . . .

I would therefore answer the question raised above as follows: *you should select as the objects of your exercise those writers of a nation who are commonly considered the best.* The bad ones do not deserve the trouble taken on their account, and you cannot learn anything from them. As to mediocre authors, we have them in such a multitude that there is no need to increase their numbers further through translation. Since good texts belong to various genres, some being historical, some poetic or oratorical, and still others philosophical, everyone should select the kinds of texts which are closest to what he wants to achieve.

A further question is: how to translate. Let us give a few main rules. (1) You should not select anything for translation if you have not yet mastered either its subject matter or its language, because you will by no means be able to express in other languages what you fail to understand. (2) You should try to render well not so much every word as rather the correct sense and the complete meaning of every sentence you translate. For although words are the carriers of understanding and although I have to take the author's intention from them, they cannot be rendered in another language with such a degree of exactness that you could follow them step by step. You should therefore (3) express everything by means of locutions that do not sound strange in your own language, but have a familiar ring to them. Every language has its own expressions, which cannot be rendered exactly in any other language. And this is where an orator must always be able to supply the equivalent which has the same weight and the same beauty as the expression in the original. Finally, you should (4) keep as much as possible all figures, all ornamental speech, even the way the original is segmented into long periods. For these in particular distinguish between the nature of one writer and of another, and you should leave to each writer his own nature, which identifies him, in the translation. Yet I would not therefore advise to leave together in one piece all the long-winded sentences of a writer which can often not be rendered into German in one sentence without creating the greatest confusion . . . No, in this case a translator is rightfully entitled to the liberty of splitting up a convoluted sentence into two, three, or more parts.

To improve your skill even more in all these things you should take translations made by other scholars and compare them with their originals. You should pay attention to everything we have required of a good translator above. You should observe where the emphasis is in the original and see whether the translator has achieved it in German as well. You should investigate the beauty and the grace of all expressions and check every sentence in the translation: does he [sic] say more or less than what the writer wanted to say; has he become too concise or too verbose, too vulgar or too noble, too flat or too lively, too clear or too obscure?

[From Johann Christoph Gottsched, *Ausführliche Redekunst, nach Anleitung der alten Griechen und Römer* (1743), in the modern reprint (Hildesheim & New York: Olms, 1973).]

Johann Jakob Bodmer, 1698-1783

The fictitious letter included here shows that in reality Bodmer deserves most of the praise which is usually lavished on Goethe and Schleiermacher as theorists of translation. He is the first to distinguish clearly "between the one manner of translating, the interpretation of thought, of content, whose goal was the 'clare et distincte percipi' which is most easily reached by means of the linguistic devices of the receiving reader, and the other manner which is directed towards the formal and individual characteristics of the original, which can be captured only by means of utter precision and the adaptation of one's own linguistic devices to what is foreign" (Senger, 68). In doing so Bodmer not only anticipates the well-known distinctions later made by Goethe and Schleiermacher, but also categories established by August Wilhelm Schlegel and, much more recently, Katharina Reiss. The attack at the end of the "letter" is directed against Gottsched.

THE NINETY-FOURTH LETTER

Dear Sir,
   One generally hears talk about the spirit of languages and the peculiar power of speech that all nations are supposed to make use of in a different way in order to express their thoughts: they are supposed to represent the beauty of any single language, and the more specific instances of beauty of this kind a language is able to exhibit, the richer it is called. If those who know languages would, therefore, concern themselves, in this present climate of general zeal to polish and enrich the newer languages, with giving to another language which lacks this or that peculiar expression or powerful locution whatever character-istic beauty a language has over another, and to deck it out with these orna-ments, this unknown treasure would soon be common to all nations, and hence every language would not only be substantially enriched; it would also come close to achieving a perfection never hoped for.
   I know of course that analogy, syntax, and similar elements do not allow themselves to be transferred from one language into another; they are, how-ever, to languages what the shell is to the kernel, whose value is never measured according to the size, the colour etc. of the shell, and their contribution to the real treasure-house of languages is therefore minimal. If one language differed

significantly from another only because it had its own way of putting sentences together and of using them in a particular way, those who know languages would find themselves badly paid indeed with the profit they could derive thereof. But there are substantial instances of special beauty in each language which deserve all attention; and they consist primarily of certain specific locutions which have been found suitable to express this thought or that. The difference between nations themselves, the countries they inhabit, their occupations, etc. determine that these locutions should differ from one language to another.

Man, who has nothing but images about him wherever he looks, from childhood on, grows used to shaping an image of a thing as soon as he thinks of it; he goes so far in this that he even makes himself an image of things he has never seen the original of, nor heard described, on the basis of those images he is already familiar with and supposes to have some similarity with the unknown. The difficulty we all encounter when, in learning philosophy, we have to think in the abstract, without the support of substantial objects, shows sufficiently how deeply this thinking in images is ingrained in the human soul. But the thinking itself is very different, according to the different occasions everyone has for shaping his concepts. Hence the peasant does not speak like the courtier, nor the soldier like the merchant. The peasant, whose house is designed for shelter only, whose food is destined to still his hunger, whose furniture is limited to the bare essentials, will therefore produce little which is elegant or dainty in his speech; his locutions will be taken from simple things, from whatever is his everyday concern. The courtier, on the other hand, who spends all his days in splendid palaces, who sees nothing else about him but art and preciosity, whose food is prepared in the most special ways to whet his appetite, and whose stomach, which is sick with looking on abundance, must be cured with foreign wines — will this lascivious and repulsive existence not fill his head in such a way that everything he says will be rich and soft, and that all his thoughts will appear in artificial images?

Whole nations are also subject to what can be observed in single individuals or classes: a rough, warlike nation and a weak, effeminate one will betray their different life-styles in their languages. Everyone admires a virile, generous nature in the English nation, which is peculiar to it and which also expresses itself in its language. It is easy to see why it has taken so many figurative expressions from blood, massacre, death, etc.: they acquire common images, easy to use, of these things which other nations abhor, by observing, from childhood on, the casual way in which suicide is treated, the general contempt for life, the many fights among men and animals. This is also the reason why an English writer of tragedies is, so to speak, under the obligation of putting the tragic ending of the story, or at least the effect thereof, on the stage before the spectator's eyes, whereas the shocked eyes and the weak heart of the French would never allow this. Where else might the figurative expressions about ships and their construction and about navigation have come from, if not from those nations who are most concerned with these occupations, who are always on ships and who therefore shape most of these concepts?

Even though a different life-style and different occupations result in the fact that people express their thoughts in different ways, this does not prevent these expressions, dissimilar though they may sound, from being powerful and easy to use, precisely because it must be presupposed that an accurate knowledge of the image which has been taken as a model produced them; especially since all figurative expressions, which, it takes little time to notice, make up the greater part of all languages, are nothing but similes; the better I know an image, the easier it will be for me to determine in how far it is suitable to give clear shape and expression to my thoughts. If I find that an expression completely exhausts the thought, that the colouring and the image a speaker makes use of to inform his neighbour of what he is thinking are so powerful and so accurate that they effect in everyone else the same ideas he himself has of something and wants to arouse in others, then I have also found in this the highest degree of the essential beauty of a language. For it is easy to see that this does not consist of empty sounds, but that it is rooted in the nature of things. That nature of things is the same in every land, but man's perception is different, as is his observation. Whoever fails to think of an appropriate word or even a decent image to express his thoughts may therefore be excused the first time, but if later he happens to find this same thought powerfully expressed in another language, be it literally or figuratively, and if he still refuses to speak that way in future, he renders himself liable to the most severe punishment. The excuse that the expression is strange to him, unheard of, etc. should not be allowed to stand; for even is he has no conception of it, he will at least find it worth his while to learn to understand the expression, and he will at least stand to gain a small enrichment of his stock of words and images; but if he understands the expression he will find that he has never yet fully grasped the thing in question, or at least not from the point of view from which he finds it now represented; he may therefore learn from it how endless representations, and hence as many expressions, may be shaped in speech on the basis of one well-known image.

Whoever undertakes an intensive study of these peculiar expressions will soon find that the number of those for which we are completely without a concept is very limited and that on the contrary most have come from those general concepts in which the nature of things instructs all men everywhere in the same way. The concept of fire, of water, of a king, etc. is the same everywhere, and everyone will therefore soon understand in his own language what the flames of love are, or the waters of sorrow, or the king of flowers, etc. Even if the image is very strange, the clear concept of the two words which have been combined cannot fail to determine the precise meaning of the whole. It is just that the qualities are adduced in a different way and that the manner in which they are represented, which is commonly called the power of speech, is not completely the same.

Those who love this true and inner ornament of language can find no better

way to acquaint themselves with the general beauty and with particular instances of it than to take the trouble of translating into their mother tongue
well-formed pieces of poetry and oratory which have been written in foreign
languages; for if they want to take care to retain accurately the thoughts of the
author in their particular power, they will soon find ample occasion to famil-
iarize themselves with the riches and the deficiencies of both languages: they
will find many locutions they understand without difficulty in the foreign
language, but when obliged to translate those same locutions into their mother
tongue they will stop short. Either the way in which the words are connected is
very unusual, or else the power of the expression strikes them as strange, or the
thought finds itself represented by an absurd and disfigured image; in a word,
they realize that they have never heard this thought expressed in this way in
their mother tongue. Yet they will not seldom happen on passages in which the
locutions will seem watery and insipid to them when compared to those in
which they usually see similar thoughts dressed. It is, however, easy to determine what is to be done; for if the intention is simply to communicate the
matter contained in the original in another language, the translator is under the
obligation to translate everything as clearly and simply as possible, according to
the spirit of his language. If, however, what is needed is an accurate translation
which not only offers the thoughts of the original but also retains all the ways
and means the author uses to express his thoughts, this must be done with
extreme precision, and one should not be afraid of being accused of unheard-
of idiosyncracies or even downright mistakes.

Just as the intentions of translators are very different, just so must the world
of necessity be full of an innumerable amount and many varieties of translations. For some time now, Germany has made it its special concern to famil-
iarize its inhabitants with the writings of antiquity and with many pieces of
recent lore via translations. Most have been satisfied with merely communicating matters treated in the original; I do not want to investigate how felicitously
all this has been done; it is enough that everything has been said in pure and
elegant German; yet very few have gone so far as to try to bring the manner in
which the foreign author presented his objects under the eyes of the German
reader. The stern rule which has been exercised so harshly by certain overlords
in the realm of the German language has marked all such attempts with its
public ridicule as with a painful iron, if it has not merely smothered them. A
general, stupid submission seemed to legitimize that tyranny.

The courage and the skill with which you, sir, have concerned yourself with
good style in so many other respects, leads me to hope that you will not deny us
your assistance, so that we shall be able to make use of natural freedom as we
see fit in this case also. We are living in a country in which we would like the
freedom of words to match the freedom of things. You have given us some
hope that you will deal with this matter. We expect it of you. Teach those
arrogant judges of language where the real value of languages lies, how their
beauty should be judged not from the spelling of words but from the perception

of things themselves, and how, consequently, whatever is beautiful in nature is beautiful everywhere, that it cannot, consequently, be beautiful in one language and left absurd in another, etc. Tell them that there is no better way to achieve that general enrichment of languages which they themselves boast of as their goal, than such teachings as are taken from the nature and qualities of things themselves. Whoever takes the trouble of literally translating a piece of writing, especially poetic writing, into his mother tongue, will be convinced of these truths by ample proof, and he will find that most locutions which seem strange and unusual to us not only have nothing indecent about them, if they are well analysed, but often represent things by means of very appropriate images and therefore arouse the reader's attention in a very special way.

[Johann Jakob Bodmer, *Der Mahler der Sitten* (1746), Ninety-Fourth Letter, as reproduced in the modern reprint (Hildesheim & New York: Olms, 1972).]

Johann Jacob Breitinger, 1701-1776

Whereas Gottsched emphasized sense over form, Breitinger wishes the translator to treat the nature and shape of the original on the same level as its
thoughts and concepts. The translation has to make the same effect on its
readers as the original makes on those who read it in the original language. For
Breitinger this does not imply metrical translations, as it will for August Wilhelm Schlegel. Since the nature and shape of the original matter as much as its
thoughts and concepts, the distinction between translation proper and imitation has to drawn more sharply.

Breitinger further requires a high degree of empathy between the translator
and the author he sets out to translate. In his view translation is, moreover,
aimed not only at those who do know the original language, but also at the
cultivated reader who knows more languages than one and is therefore able to
compare the original with various translations. This cultivated reader has
become a rarity in our time, but he still plays a very important part in
Schleiermacher's theory of translation.

Breitinger's chosen model of literary excellence was Milton, not French
neo-classicism, which rendered a polemic with Gottsched inevitable. Both he
and Bodmer subscribed to a theory of language based on a rather naïve concept
of universality which was to be revived, in a more complex form, by transfor-
mational generative linguists in our century.

His "empathy requirement", his insistence on treating form on the same
level as content, and the subsequent sharp distinction between translation and
imitation, or version, still hold good in our time, as does his concept of the
translator as a man of taste, who selects the best in foreign literatures and
incorporates them into his own.

EQUIVALENCE

Many others before me have considered translation a very useful exercise
which enables you to acquire, almost unnoticed, the ability to think rightly and
to express your thoughts with emphasis and to your advantage . . . That is why
this exercise has, in all times, been considered an easy and reliable method to
transmit good taste in the rhetorical arts and to increase the wealth of a
language. The matter of the previous chapter made me decide to treat the art of

translation separately, because it made me think that really equivalent words can only be found in different languages. You should therefore look on different languages as on so many collections of totally equivalent words and locutions which are interchangeable, and which fully correspond to each other in meaning, since they diverge from each other only in their external sound and shape.

Languages are ways through which men can reveal their thoughts: since the objects men deal with in their thoughts are one and the same in the whole world, since the truth they search for by means of this activity is of one kind only, and since all man's emotional powers are limited in the same way, it follows that there must be, of necessity, a certain equivalence in men's thoughts — which is why that equivalence also becomes a necessity in the expressions of those thoughts.

The whole art of translating from one language into another rests on this basis. A translator is required to express the same thoughts and concepts he finds before him — arranged in an excellent pattern — in the same arrangement, with the same combination and coherence, and with similar emphasis, in other, equivalent signs accepted by, used by, and known to a nation, so that the concept or thought underlying both signs makes the same impression on the reader's feelings. Translation is like painting a portrait: the more it looks like the original, the more praise it deserves. Therefore the translator must impose the following harsh law upon himself: that he will never take the liberty to deviate from the original, whether with respect to the thoughts expressed in it, or to their nature and shape. These must remain unchanged to the same degree of light and strength, and only their signs may be exchanged for equivalent signs. In translation Milton should present us with exactly the same noble and marvelous images and descriptions arranged in the same order as in the original, and he must arouse in the heart of the German reader the same high concepts and changing moods that reader would observe and experience if the signs in which the expression is clothed in English were known to him.

These are the thoughts that Flaccus [Quintus Horatius Flaccus, or Horace] casually expressed in his *Poetics* with these words: "Nec verbum verbo curabis reddere fidus / Interpres" [And do not strive to render word for word, faithful translator] — for one should take these words in their context. Horace wants to show here how big the difference is that separates a free imitation from a bound translation. As far as translation goes he defines the translator's duties in these words: "ut verbum verbo curet reddere" [let him take care to render word for word]; to the imitation, on the other hand, he allows more freedom, where he says explicitly that these two exercises, which are totally different, should not be confused with each other. It is therefore totally absurd, and totally opposed to the opinion of this poet who was engaged in teaching his art, when this line is often quoted in such a way as to suggest that the translator is given the advice not to stick too closely to the expressions of his original, but to take the liberty of moving away from them as he pleases, as long as he gives us similar thoughts to understand. This interpretation ascribes a meaning to Horace which he not only abhors with arid words, but which is also in contradiction to the nature and the aims of a translation, since these are to produce the same thoughts and concepts and the same impressions in the reader's heart, in the same number, measure, and force, by means of the mere substitution of equivalent signs. Since no well-written manuscript contains a single superfluous word which could be omitted without changing it and impairing its clarity, emphasis, or ornamentation; since rather, each word has its necessary reason for being in the author's intention which it is designed to serve in a certain way, the translator must weigh all the words and expressions of the original with great care, and not omit any of the concepts which are linked with them, but express them in his translation with the same degree of clarity and emphasis, by means of equivalent words.

This translator's work is, to be sure, not as easy as one is wont to imagine. It presupposes, first, that the translator should have good taste, so that he can recognize and discern excellent originals which, more than others, are worth the trouble of translating, as regards both inventiveness and expression, for this choice allows us to see in advance, so to speak, to what extent we can trust his ability and his skill. Second, that the translator should know the language he wants to translate from, that he should possess common sense, and that he should think in exactly the same way as the original author, to the extent that he acquires a clear and sufficient insight into the perfection of his original. Since this perfection rests on the artistic combination of various intentions, the translator must, once he has understood these intentions, be able to account precisely for the nature, force, and necessity of the different images and other components within the limits imposed on them. This implies that before he sets to work the translator should find himself in the same situation in which the original author must have been when he arranged his work in the right order in his mind and when he reached the stage at which he could share it with the imaginative powers of his readers by means of sound expression.

Whoever thinks these preparations are not too difficult, and whoever would like to consider the art of translation in isolation, as merely a substitution of equivalent signs, ought to be reminded of two factors which render this task difficult. First, that no equivalent words and locutions one can freely chose from are to be found in a language: there is, therefore, not a variety of expressions which corresponds to a certain and fully defined thought, but just one. It is not so easy to hit on the right expression, especially not in a language which has not yet been fully developed. Second, that every language has its own very special character, which differentiates it from every other language; it is therefore often hard for the translator to express the thoughts of his original without loss of emphasis and beauty in equivalent signs which even so do not sound strange in his own language, and do not do violence to its character.

A good translator must have mastered to perfection the nature, the constitution, and the ways of the language he wants to translate into, and he must take great pains to incorporate them into his translation as best he can, especially so when he is forced to deviate from his original because of a certain idiom in it: this is the only way in which he can give his translation the character and appearance of an original. A translator should also be more careful in his work, because he is faced with the disadvantage that the reader who knows both languages will put copy and original side by side and will be able to find out how closely he has hit his mark or how far he has fallen short of it, whereas it is not so easy to decide in the work of the original writer whether the mistakes in his writing are caused by a lack of ability to think or by lack of knowledge of the language.

This seems to tell us why so many German translations have gone wrong in the past. The reason is, in my opinion, not so much to be found in any inability on the translator's part, but rather in an exaggerated conception of the superfluous abundance of the German language, in pernicious prejudices concerning equivalent words and locutions, and above all in the misunderstanding of a faithful translator's duties and the excessive liberty taken to deviate from the original. I might add that there are a few who are led even farther astray from the original because they have taken upon themselves the yoke of German metre and rhyme even though they have, at the same time, taken unlimited liberties.

[From Johann Jacob Breitinger, *Critische Dichtkunst* (1740), in the modern reprint (Stuttgart: Metzler, 1966).]

Gotthold Ephraim Lessing, 1729-1781

Lessing introduces a number of new topics. He is concerned with the specific nature of the original, which should not be mangled in the translation, even though he is, by modern standards, not very consistent in his judgment: Pope should not be translated into prose, but Pindar may be. He assesses the relative merits of commentary and translation, and judges commentary inferior. He emphasizes that there is no difference between the translator and the writer of the original, another truth still not commonly accepted in the twentieth century. He deplores the commercialization of translation, which is on the increase in our time, points to the damage bad translators can do, and draws attention to the translator's responsibility in shaping the canon of world literature.

Lessing also strongly voices his anti-French sentiments as well as his opposition to Gottsched. He ridicules those who have taken Gottsched's exhortation to translate as an "exercise" too literally. Yet he agrees with Gottsched on the necessity of critical writing on translation.

The "you" in the extracts that follow is the imaginary army captain to whom Lessing addressed his imaginary letters on contemporary literature. He has been away to the wars for a number of years and wants to be brought up to date on the literature produced in his absence.

GENRE

As a trade, learning at least is plied among us with passable assiduity. The sales registers have not grown much smaller and our translators are still beavering away with great enthusiasm. What have they not already translated and what will they not translate! I happen to have a translation in front of me right now. The translator has applied himself to an English poet. Guess whom? You'll never guess. Pope.

And he has translated him into prose. A poet whose great, not to say greatest merit lay in what we call the mechanics of poetry, whose whole endeavour was to put the richest, most poignant sense into the fewest, most melodious words; to whom rhyme was not a matter to be trifled with. To translate such a poet into prose is to disfigure him in a worse way than Euclid would be disfigured if he were translated into verse.

It was the bookseller's idea, of course. The translator himself admits it. And what does it matter to him how the bookseller allows him to make money, and how he wants to make his money himself?

Our translators rarely know the language [of the original]; they want to learn it; they translate as an exercise and they are smart enough to get themselves paid for their exercises. They are even less able to think along with their original. For if they were not totally incapable of doing so, they would nearly always be able to spot from the way the argument is conducted where their imperfect knowledge of the language has led them to make mistakes.

You are right; bad translations of the kind I have introduced you to are below all criticism. Yet it is a good thing when criticism stoops down to them once in a while, for the damage they do is indescribable. If, suddenly, through a great, mysterious change in the world, all books would disappear except those written in German, what a poor figure Virgil and Horace, Shaftesbury and Bolingbroke would cut for posterity!

"Nobody", say the authors of the *Bibliothek* [the *Bibliothek der schönen Wissenschaften und freien Künste,* a periodical founded by Bodmer in 1759] "will deny that the German theatre owes a great deal of its early improvement to Herr Professor Gottsched."

I am that nobody. I utterly deny it. It would have been better if Herr Gottsched had never dabbled in the theatre. His so-called improvements are either concerned with superfluous trivialities, or else they make matters much worse. When Frau Neuber [Caroline Neuber, who with her husband headed a troupe of actors at the Brunswick court] flourished, and so many felt the call to do well by her and the theatre, our dramatic literature was in wretched straits, to be sure. Rules were unknown; nobody cared about models. Our heroic and political actions were full of nonsense, bombast, low humour, and dirt. Our comedies consisted of tricks and disguises; fights were the pinnacles of their wit. You did not have to be the finest and noblest of minds to diagnose this depravity. Therefore Herr Gottsched was not the first to do this; he was merely the first to credit himself with enough skill to remedy the situation. And how did he do it? He knew a little French and began to translate. He urged everybody who was able to turn a rhyme and understand *Oui Monsieur* to do the same thing . . . in short, he was not satisfied with wanting to improve our old theatre; he also wanted to create a completely new one. What kind? The frenchifying kind — and he did not take the trouble to investigate whether this frenchifying theatre was suitable to the German way of thinking or not.

TRANSLATION AND COMMENTARY

Pindar has truly roused a bold young mind in Switzerland, who wants to improve our understanding of the Theban singer's enthusiasm. This is a very difficult thing to do; it is incomparably easier to write a learned commentary on the whole of Pindar than to translate a single ode well. But our young Swiss [Johann Jacob Steinbrüchel] thinks along with his poet, and his attempt has turned out to be very successful indeed. A friend has given it to me; let me, in turn, give it to you.

I know you would not expect the translation to be in verse. The Germans alone, I am almost tempted to say, are at liberty to make their prose as poetic as they want it to be; and since they can be most faithful in this poetic prose, why should they impose the yoke of metre upon themselves, if they can no longer be faithful under it?

THE BEST TRANSLATOR

The author [Johann Nikolaus Meinhard] of the *Versuche über den Charakter und die Werke der besten italienischen Dichter* [Essays on the Nature and Works of the Best Italian Poets, 1763-1764] is a man who awakens our feelings of real respect. We lacked a work of this kind, and we could wish, but hardly hope, to see it written with such taste. He is the best translator, if someone who gives proof of such a thorough acquaintance with all the most excellent men of genius of a whole nation, who combines such fine feeling with such right judgment, under whose touch such manifold beauties are given a radiance, a life which rivals the flowering with which they shine forth on their native soil, in a language for which they did not in the least seem intended; if, I say, such a poet may be called a translator at all; if he is not rather an original writer himself who would not be lacking in inventiveness if he had not wanted to divest himself of it, to our advantage.

It would be true to say that Italian literature has not really ever become widely known among us . . . The contents of these *Essays* will, therefore, also possess the merit of the new for most readers, and our brighter minds will discover completely unknown lands and shores in them and be able to include them in their literary commerce to great advantage.

Or do you think that this worthy man has a predilection for Italians? You are mistaken; he has to be acquainted with English literature to the same extent. For to him we also owe the translation of Henry Howe's *Principles of Criticism*. Yet here the man of taste had to enter into an alliance with the philosopher, all in the person of the translator. I did not know to which of our translators I should look for this combination. A completely unknown name has solved that riddle. You are glad; yet you are amazed at the same time. Remember what Seneca says: "Some are famous, others ought to be."

[All extracts from Gotthold Ephraim Lessing, *Briefe, die neueste Literatur betreffend* (1759-1765), as reprinted in GEL, *Gesammelte Werke* (Leipzig: Tempel, 1912).]

Johann Gottfried Herder, 1744-1803

With Herder the tradition shifts gears: "Herder expressed only very general thoughts; or rather, he used translation to illustrate his total way of thinking..." (Fränzel, 155). Translation is no longer a literary and/or linguistic activity. It becomes a metaphor, a category of thought, and will remain so in the work of the "masters". The divine is trans-lated into the human in language. The spirit of the infinite reveals itself in all languages and all poetry – an idea later to be taken up again by Benjamin. Actual translation is a pale reflection of this.

Every living language is a mother tongue, and therefore unique, and therefore not inferior to any other. German is, in other words, the equal of French, if not its superior. "This front position against the French language was taken up again by the early Romantics and reinforced until it became a grotesque miscalculation, for if one wanted to purify German into the language of poetry, and consequently the language of translation as such, one had to eliminate the keenest competition as soon as possible ..." (Huyssen, 33).

To improve the German language Herder favours purely linguistic imports, preferably from the classics. Equivalent locutions are not enough. The actual linguistic material must be cast in a foreign mould. The danger is obvious: the translation may adapt itself to the foreign model to such an extent that it is no longer recognizable as German. Both Schleiermacher and Benjamin were to succumb to it.

Herder stresses the importance of philological knowledge (the translator should be a philosopher, a poet, and a philologist) and attacks the type of pedanticism which had, since Gottsched, found an outlet in interminable and superfluous (foot)notes – a phenomenon by no means totally extinct in twentieth-century translations. By stating that a translation should do well by one language and bear fruit in another, Herder lifts the fidelity/freedom debate onto a higher level.

His view of language, which he had in part inherited from the irrationalist philosopher Johann Georg Hamann, and his insistence that all reading is translation, meant a new departure for the tradition. "It is obvious and needs no special mention that the breakthrough of the new theory [with Schleiermacher] took place after the new theories of language and literature had been added as most important components, according to which the holy original text of the creator-author could take the place of the holy text of the Bible ..." (Senger, 87).

TRANSLATION AS "IMPROVEMENT"

The real translator should therefore adapt words, ways of speech, and combinations from a more developed language to his mother tongue. Preferably from Greek and Latin, and also from younger languages... All older languages have, like older nations and their works, more characteristic traits than those which are newer. Our language should therefore be able to learn more from them than from languages it claims close kinship with; or else the difference between the two will at least provide philosophers of language with a wealth of material for further observation.

Homer, Aeschylus, Sophocles created beauty for a language which did not yet possess a developed prose style. Let their translator plant that beauty in a language which remains prose even when it is written in metre, even − as we believe to have proved − in the hexameter. And let him do it in such a way that the loss is as small as possible. They clothed thoughts in words and feelings in images; the translator has to be a creative genius himself if he wants to be of service to his author and his language. A German Homer, Aeschylus, Sophocles, as classical in German as they are in Greek, builds a monument unnoticed by pedants and schoolmasters, but it holds the eye of the wise by virtue of its silent grandeur and simple splendour and deserves the inscription "Sacred to eternity and to those who come after". Such a translator is without a doubt many heads higher than another who translates from an epoch closer to us in time, a language more akin to ours, a nation which shares our way of thinking and our genius, a work written in the lightest poetic tone, the didactic, and which nonetheless loses most of its colour in translation.

TRANSLATION AND EXPLICATION: CONTEXT

We should definitely not waste our time on wretched imitations, and a writer like [Ludwig Friedrich] Hudemann in his *Luzifer* [Lucifer, 1765] and his *Brudermord des Kains* (Cain's Fratricide, 1765] is not worth noticing and being irritated by. But how can we get rid of such Hudemanns? We must find the courage to study Hebrew poems as poems, we must learn to explain them and we must make them known. It is impossible for us to translate them and to imitate them before we understand them, and Semitic philology, which has been flourishing in Germany for some time, will, if it allies itself with taste, scatter bad and stupid imitators.

The best translator must be the best explicator; if only the reverse were true, and if they could both come together, we could soon hope for a book with the following title: "A Poetic Translation of Hebrew Poems, Explained in the Context of the Country, the History, the Opinions, the Religion, the Situation, the Customs, and the Language of Their Nation and Transplanted into the Genius of Our Time, Our Thinking, and Our Language". It would be possible to state truthfully in the preface: "This translation was of necessity a very difficult and laborious piece of work, the more so since the remarks of a few philologists of taste and [Johann Andreas] Cramer's Psalms [1755-1764] have been capable only of making a small contribution in the field of explication and translation respectively — they have been of help at times: they have drawn our attention to different points of view and kept us on our guard. But we think of this as an original work which could exert a greater influence on literature than ten original works. It draws the boundary lines between foreign nations and ourselves, no matter how convoluted those lines may be; it makes us more familiar with the beauty and genius of a nation we are used to observe from afar only, and yet we ought to know it face to face: it is a model of an imitation which manages to remain original. Even if it is not blessed with the good fortune of engendering new, really new men of genius, it will at least grow into a wall of thorns in the path of the lackeys and lovers of foreign idols, and make them lose their way. It will seize them, pull them back and say: 'Look, this is your nature and this is your history, here are your idols, here is your world, your philosophy, your language: model yourself on these, and become your own imitator.' And should you want to make use of the treasures of one of the most excellent nations: look, they are here. I want to teach you their art of trans-forming history and religion into poetry; do not steal what they have invented; steal their art of inventing, of creation, of expression."

Where is there a translator who is at the same time a philosopher, a poet, and a philologist: he is to be the morning star of a new era in our literature.

PEDANTICISM AND COMMERCIALIZATION

A second, higher level: if we could find translators who would not just study their author with a view to translating the sense of the original into our language, "but who would also be able to find his distinctive tone of voice, to take over the nature of his style and to express for us the really distinctive features, the diction and the colouring of the foreign original, its dominant traits, its genius and the nature of its poetic style". This is, of course, very much to ask for, and yet not enough to meet my ideal of the translator. Most translators love to throw a word in edgewise, in the preface, in the notes, or in their author's *vita*. Most of them scatter compliments in the preface, or speak of editions used. In the notes, on the other hand, they often give boring explana-tions which do not credit the reader with common sense, or else recriminations which fail to arouse his interest, or even a mishmash of philological pedanti-cism. Last but not least they top all this with a translation of the author's life. The book is made: for the translator it is his bread and butter; for the publisher an article to sell in the market-place, for the buyer a book in his library. For literature? Nothing! Or even a negative contribution. Zero or less than zero.

TRANSLATION OF A CULTURE

And the translation? It should not be embellished, of course. The French, who are overproud of their national taste, adapt all things to it, rather than to try to adapt themselves to the taste of another time. Homer must enter France a captive, and dress according to fashion, so as not offend their eye. He has to allow them to take his venerable beard and his old simple clothes away from him. He has to conform to French customs, and where his peasant coarseness still shows he is ridiculed as a barbarian. But we poor Germans, who still are almost an audience without a fatherland, who are still without tyrants in the field of national taste, we want to see him the way he is.

And the best translation cannot achieve this for Homer without the help of notes and explanations in the highest critical spirit. We would be glad to travel with the translator if he were to take us to Greece and show us the treasures he has found. Since we are not very used to this kind of travelling, since we are even vaguely repelled by it, he should direct our attention, he should guide us as customers who are not interested in the stories of schoolboys and the thieving of words, but in the awesome secrets of state which abound in Greek literature. We know what notes on the classics after the French taste are like: they usually dismember, one by one, beautiful features, often rather trivial in nature, which have been written to provide the audience with relaxation, pleasure, and recreation. We know how pedants annotate the classics. We also know Grimm's notes on Anacreon and [Johann Arnold] Ebert's notes on [Edward] Young [in his translation of the English poet's *Night Thoughts*, 1754]. We can therefore extrapolate full sunlight from this dawn; we can see how an audience could be educated in the Greek taste by Homer. I should not like to think that poetry and hexameters should be lacking in this translation; but they should be poetry and hexameters in the Greek taste, even if they only serve to draw our attention to the extent to which our language and poetry lag behind.

IRRELEVANT CRITICISM

How easily our bread-and-butter reviewers take translators to task with great severity and point out linguistic mistakes. The finest criticism is, in my opinion, that which is able to show exactly where the boundary line runs, how a translator should not get a hair's breadth too close to either of his languages, the one he translates from or the one he translates into. Too lax a translation, which our surveyors of art are in the habit of calling free and natural, sins against both: it does not do well by one language, it does not bear fruit in another. Too adaptive a translation is a much more difficult enterprise, even though light, frivolous minds decry it as servile: it does well by its languages and is rarely awarded the recognition it deserves. Because this kind of translator must attempt, adapt, dare all the time, our censors of the raised eyebrow reward him by decrying his work because of three attempts that have gone wrong, by taking all his bold experiments for linguistic mistakes and by treating an artist's endeavours as they would a schoolboy's homework.

READING IS TRANSLATION

When I read Homer I have no choice but to become a Greek, whichever way I
read him; so why not in my mother tongue. I secretly have to read him like that
anyway — the reader's soul secretly translates him for itself, wherever it can do
so, even if it hears him in Greek: and I, sensuous reader! I cannot imagine any
really useful and vivid reading of Homer without this secret translation. I read
as if I were hearing him only when I translate him: he sings to me in Greek and
my German thoughts try to follow his flight as quickly, as nobly, as harmo-
niously; then, and then only, am I able to render a precise and vivid account of
Homer to myself and others, and to feel him with all my soul. In all other cases
one reads him, I believe, as a commentator, an annotator, a schoolmaster, or a
learner of languages, and this kind of reading is vague or dead. To understand
Homer is one thing, says Winckelmann [Johann Joachim Winckelmann, the
archeologist and art historian], to be able to explain him to yourself another;
and this happens in my soul only by means of a secret translation, a rapid
change in thought and language.

That language is, moreover, much more suited to become Homer's translator
than French is, or English. German alone could possibly find a middle way
between paraphrase and schoolboy translation — for that is what most French
translations are. And this middle way could be referred to by means of an old
German word, the emphatic use of which has become contemptible and ridiculous to us because it has been wrongly used so often: germanization. Of course
I shall go on studying Homer in the original, even if Meinhard were to translate
him; it is just that I would not be ashamed to have the translation lie next to that
original, to look at, to compete with, whenever there is a strong image I want to
feel fully in my mother tongue — that is how I read Homer.

[All extracts from Johann Gottfried Herder, *Fragmente* (1766-1767), as reprinted in JGH, *Sämtliche
Werke* (Berlin: Weidmannsche Buchhandlung, 1877).]

Johann Wolfgang Goethe, 1749-1832

Following Herder, Goethe introduces an evolutionary component into the tradition. Rules for the production of a "good" translation can no longer be absolute, because the "good" translation itself is no longer absolute. Whether a translation is "good" or not depends on the stage that has been reached in the relationship between source literature and target literature.

Goeth's third type of translation, which he does not endorse without certain reservations, becomes Schleiermacher's ideal, just as the distinction Goethe makes between leaving the author alone and moving the reader towards him, and *vice versa*, reappears at the core of Schleiermacher's essay. Benjamin later tries to extend the third type to languages as such, rather than works of literature.

Goethe widens the horizon of the tradition by extending translation to works taken from the literatures Western Europe considered (and still considers) exotic. He lifts translation beyond its purely esthetic dimension by stating that the aim of translating literature is to increase tolerance among nations. His idea of what is now called a "clearing-house" for translations, some kind of body which would suggest what works ought to be translated, has not as yet been realized.

THE THREE EPOCHS OF TRANSLATION

There are three kinds of translation. The first acquaints us with foreign countries on our own terms; a simple prosaic translation is best in this respect. For since prose totally cancels all peculiarities of any kind of poetic art, and since prose itself pulls poetic enthusiasm down to a common water-level, it does the greatest service in the beginning, by surprising us with foreign excellence in the midst of our national homeliness, our everyday existence; it offers us a higher mood and real edification while we do not realize what is happening to us. Luther's Bible translation will produce this kind of effect at any time.

If the *Nibelungen* had been put into decent prose at the outset, and if it had been stamped a popular romance, much would have been gained and the singular, dark, noble, awesome sense of chivalry would have addressed itself to us with its full strenght. Whether this is still advisable or feasible now will best be judged by those who have applied themselves more thoroughly to these matters of great antiquity.

A second epoch follows in which [the translator] really only tries to appropriate foreign content and to reproduce it in his own sense, even though he tries to transport himself into foreign situations. I would like to call this kind of epoch the parodistic one, in the fullest sense of that word. In most cases men of wit feel called to this kind of trade. The French use this method in their translations of all poetic works; hundreds of examples can be found in the translations produced by [Abbé Jacques] Delille [a well-known and prolific French translator of the day]. Just as the French adapt foreign words to their pronunciation, just so do they treat feelings, thoughts, even objects; for every foreign fruit they demand a counterfeit grown in their own soil.

Wieland's translations are of this kind; he too had a singular sense of understanding and taste which brought him close to antiquity and to foreign countries only to the extent to which he could still feel comfortable. This excellent man may be considered the representative of his time; he has had an extraordinary impact, precisely because what he found pleasing, how he appropriated it, and how he communicated it in his turn seemed pleasing and enjoyable also to his contemporaries.

Since it is impossible to linger too long either in the perfect or in the imperfect and one change must of necessity follow another, we experienced the third epoch, which is to be called the highest and the final one, namely the one in which the aim is to make the original identical with the translation, so that one would not be valued instead of the other, but in the other's stead.

This kind had to overcome the greatest resistance originally; for the translator who attaches himself closely to his original more or less abandons the originality of his nation, and so a third comes into existence, and the taste of the multitude must first be shaped towards it.

Voss [Johann Heinrich Voss, the translator of Homer into hexameters], who will never be praised enough, could not satisfy the public initially; yet slowly, bit by bit, it listened itself into his new manner and made itself comfortable in it. But whoever can now see what has happened, what versatility has come to the Germans, what rhetorical, rhythmical, metrical advantages are at the disposal of the talented and knowledgeable youngster, how Ariosto and Tasso, Shakespeare and Calderón are now presented to us twice and three times over as germanized foreigners, may hope that literary history will plainly state who was the first to take this road in spite of so many obstacles.

The works of von Hammer [the Viennese Orientalist Joseph von Hammer-Purgstall] point for the most part to a similar treatment of Oriental masterpieces, in which approximation to the external form is to be most recommended. The passages of a translation of Firdausi which our friend has given us reveal themselves as endlessly more profitable when compared to those of an adaptor whom we can read excerpts of in the *Fundgruben* [*des Orients,* a review of Oriental studies edited by von Hammer]. Adapting a poet in this way is, in my opinion, the saddest mistake a diligent translator, who is moreover well-suited to his taks, could make. But since these three epochs are repeated and inverted in every literature; since, indeed, these three methods can be applied simultaneously, a translation into prose of the *Shàh-náma* [Book of Kings, the Persian poet Firdausi's long poem] and the works of Nizāmī is still in order. It could be used for rapid reading which would open up the main sense; we would be pleased with the historical, the legendary, and the generally ethical and we would move closer and closer to moods and ways of thought, until we could totally fraternize with them at last.

Remember the most resolute recognition we Germans have given such a translation of the *Sakuntalà* [by the Indian dramatist Kâlidâsa]; we can ascribe its great impact to the general prose in which the poem has been diluted. But it is about time now for someone to offer it to us in a translation of the third type, which would correspond to the different dialects as well as to the rhythmical, metrical, and prosaic ways of speech in the original, and which would allow us to enjoy that poem anew in all its idiosyncrasy and to naturalize it for us. Since a manuscript of this eternal work may be found in Paris, a German who lives there could gain undying merit among us if he were to undertake such a work.

The English translator of [Kâlidâsa's] *Messenger of the Clouds*, or *Meghadûta* [Horace H. Wilson] is also worthy of all praise, because the first acquaintance with such a work is always momentous in one's life. But his translation really belongs in the second period, in that it is suppletory and paraphrastic; it flatters the Northeasterly ear and senses through the iambic pentameter. I am indebted to our Kosegarten [Ludwig Gotthard Kosegarten, a scholar-author of the time] for a few lines translated directly from the original language, and they give a totally different impression indeed. The Englishman has, moreover, allowed himself transpositions of motifs which the trained esthetic eye immediately discovers and disapproves of. It remains to explain in a few words why we called the third epoch the final one. A translation which attempts to identify itself with the original in the end comes close to an interlinear version and greatly enhances our understanding of the original; this in turn leads us, compels us as it were, towards the source text, and so the circle is closed at last. Inside it the coming together of the foreign and the native, the unknown approximation and the known, keep moving towards each other.

[From Johann Wolfgang Goethe, *West-Östlicher Divan* (1819), as reprinted in JWG, *Werke* (Hamburg: Wegener, 1967).]

THE PEDAGOGICAL VALUE OF PROSE TRANSLATIONS

Wieland's translation [of Shakespeare] appeared. It was devoured, shared with and recommended to friends and acquaintances. We Germans had the advantage that many important works of foreign nations were first translated in a light and bantering vein. The translations of Shakespeare in prose, first Wieland's, then [Johann Joachim] Eschenburg's, could quickly spread as reading matter. They were generally intelligible and suited to the common reader. I honour both rhythm and rhyme, through which poetry becomes poetry indeed, but what is really deeply and thoroughly operative, what really shapes and improves, is what is left of a poet when he has been translated into prose. What remains then is the pure, perfect essence which a blinding exterior often succeeds in deluding us with when it is not there, and in hiding when it is. That is why I think translations into prose are more advantageous than translations into verse in the first stages of education; one can see that boys, who turn everything into a joke, make fun of the sound of words, the fall of syllables, and destroy the deep essence of the noblest work out of a certain sense of parodistic devilry. I should therefore like you to consider whether we are not in need of a prose translation of Homer; it should, of course, be worthy of the level that German literature has reached by now. I leave this and what I said before to the consideration of our worthy pedagogues who can rely on extensive experience in this matter. I simply want to remind you of Luther's Bible translation as an argument in favour of my proposal. That this excellent man offered us in our mother tongue, and as it were in one piece, a work written in the most different styles, as well as its poetic, historical, imperative, didactic tone, has helped religion more than if he had aspired to recreate the idiosyncracies of that original down to the smallest detail. Later translators have tried in vain to make us enjoy the book of Job, the Psalms, and other canticles in their poetic form. If you want to influence the masses, a simple translation is always best. Critical translations vying with the original are really of use only for conversations conducted by the learned among themselves.

[From Johann Wolfgang Goethe, *Dichtung und Wahrheit* (1811-1814), as reprinted in JWG, *Werke* (Hamburg: Wegener, 1967).]

IN PRAISE OF THE TRANSLATOR

If we can put ourselves immediately into such a distant stituation, with no knowledge of local colour and without understanding the language, if we can observe a foreign literature at our ease, without previous historical research, if we can bring to mind the taste of a certain time, the meaning and the genius of a nation, whom should we give thanks to but the translator who has exercised his talents with great diligence for our benefit, his whole life long . . . Hail therefore to the translator, who focused his powers on one spot, who moved in one single direction, that we might enjoy a thousandfold.

A truly general tolerance will most certainly be reached if you respect the particular characteristics of single individuals and nations; you should, however, keep in mind while you translate that what has real merit distinguishes itself in that it belongs to humanity as a whole. Germans have contributed to such a mediation and mutual recognition. Those who understand and study German find themselves on the market-place where all nations offer their wares; they act as interpreters by enriching themselves.

And that is how we should look upon every translator, as on a man who tries to be a mediator in this general spiritual commerce and who has chosen it as his trade to advance the interchange. For whatever one may say about the deficiencies of translation, it is and remains one of the most important and dignified enterprises in the general commerce of the world. The Koran says: "God has given every nation a prophet in its own language." Thus every translator is a prophet among his people. Luther's translation of the Bible has had the most gigantic impact, even though critics still, to this very day, find fault with it and express their reservations about it.

[From Johann Wolfgang Goethe, *Schriften zur Literatur*, as reprinted in JWG, *Werke* (Hamburg: Wegener, 1967).]

TRANSLATION AS DISCOVERY OF THE FOREIGN

When you translate you should go as far as the untranslatable; then you catch sight of the foreign language and the foreign nation for the first time.

Translators should be looked upon as busy matchmakers who advertise a half-veiled beauty as being very lovely: they arouse an irresistible desire for the original.

[From Johann Wolfgang Goethe, *Maximen und Reflexionen* (1826), as reprinted in JWG, *Werke* (Hamburg: Wegener, 1967).]

AUTHOR, READER, TRANSLATOR: THE TWO MAXIMS

There are two maxims in translation: one requires that the author of a foreign nation be brought across to us in such a way that we can look on him as ours; the other requires that we should go accross to what is foreign and adapt ourselves to its conditions, its use of language, its peculiarities. The advantages of both are sufficiently known to educated people through perfect examples. Our friend, who looked for the middle way in this, too, tried to reconcile both, but as a man of feeling and taste he preferred the first maxim when in doubt.

[From Johann Wolfgang Goethe, "Zum brüderlichen Andenken Wielands" (1813), as reprinted in JWG, *Werke* (Hamburg: Wegener, 1967).]

Wilhelm von Humboldt, 1767-1835

Humboldt is among the first to realize that a language rests on the consensus of its speakers, that it is not an abstract set of words and rules. The word itself is not a mere sign to him, but a symbol, which expresses the close identity between sign and concept. Equivalents for symbols can be found in different languages, whereas it is impossible, as Schopenhauer was to point out, to find equivalents for signs expressing concepts.

Like most authors represented in this collection, Humboldt is neither very consistent nor very systematic. All languages are adequate to their purpose, yet some are better, when measured against a classical standard introduced from the outside. Hence German is a "super-language" because the metres of antiquity can be recreated in it.

Humboldt makes a number of important points: he stresses fidelity to the whole of the text, as opposed to the atomization which results from blind fidelity to parts and details. He emphasizes the importance of form in the shaping of a tradition. He reaffirms the necessity for empathy between the translator and the author he wants to translate, distinguishes between translation and commentary, and asserts that translation proceeds from inspiration, just as original writing does. Finally, he welcomes a variety of translations. Many translations result, in the end, in a cumulative approximation to the original.

A THEORY OF TRANSLATION

Such a poem [as Aeschylus' *Agamemnon*] is, because of its peculiar nature, untranslatable, in a sense vastly different from that in which such a statement is made about all works of great originality. It has often been said, and confirmed by both experience and research, that, if one excepts those expressions which designate purely physical objects, no word in one language is completely equivalent to a word in another. Different languages are, in this respect, but collections of synonyms; each expresses the concept a little differently, with such and such a denotation, each places it on a rung higher or lower on the ladder of feeling. A collection of the synonyms of the main languages, or even only of Greek, Latin, and German (which would be an eminently grateful undertaking) has never yet been attempted, even though fragmentary attempts are to be found in the works of many writers, but if it were undertaken in the right spirit it should become one of the most attractive tasks. A word is not a mere sign for a concept, since a concept cannot come into being, let alone be recorded, without the help of a word; the indeterminate activity of the power of thinking condenses into a word, just as light clouds originate in a blue sky. It has now become an individual being, with a certain character and a certain shape, with a power that influences the emotions, and not without the ability to procreate. If you were to think of the origin of a word in human terms (which is plainly impossible, merely because the act of pronouncing a word also pre-supposes the certainty of being understood, and because language itself can only be thought of as a product of simultaneous interaction, in which one is not able to help the other, but in which everybody simultaneously has to carry in himself his own work and that of all others), that origin would be analogous to the origin of an ideal shape in the imagination of an artist. This, too, cannot be drawn from what is real, it originates from a pure energy of the mind and, in the purest sense of the word, from nothing; from that moment on, however, it enters life and is now real and lasting. What man has not — even outside the field of artistic production, or the production of genius — created shapes of fantasy for himself, often in early childhood, and what man has not often lived with them more intimately than with the shapes of reality? How, therefore, could a word whose meaning is not immediately given through the senses be totaly identical with a word in another language? It must, of necessity, exhibit differences, and if one makes a precise comparison of the best, the most careful, the most faithful translations, one is amazed at the difference that is there, where the translator merely tried to preserve equivalence and identity. It could even be contended that the more a translation strives after fidelity, the more deviant it becomes. For then it also tries to imitate fine peculiarities; it avoids mere generalities and can, in any case, do little more than match each peculiar trait with a different one. Yet this should not deter us from translating. On the contrary, translation, and especially the translation of poets, is one of the most necessary tasks in a literature, partly because it brings forms of art and human life that would otherwise have remained totally unknown to those who do not know a language, and partly also, and above all, to increase the significance and the expressiveness of one's own language. For it is a marvelous character-istic of language that they all first reach into usual habits of life, and that they can afterwards endlessly be heightened, through the spirit of the nation which shapes them, to something nobler and more complex. It is not too bold a contention that everything, the highest and the deepest, the strongest and the most tender, can be expressed in every language, even in the dialects of very primitive peoples, which we do not know well enough (yet this should not be taken to mean that one language is not better than another, originally, or that some other languages are forever out of reach). It is just that these tones slumber as in an instrument that is not played, until the nation knows how to elicit them. All signs of language are symbols, not the things themselves, not signs agreed on, but sounds which find themselves, together with the things and concepts they represent, through the mind in which they originated and keep originating, in a real and, so to speak, mystical connection which the objects of reality contain as it were dissolved in ideas. These symbols can be changed, defined, separated and united in a manner for which no limit can be imagined. A higher, deeper, or more tender sense may be imputed to these symbols, which happens only if one thinks, expresses, receives, and represents them in a certain way; and so language is heightened to a nobler sense, extended into a medium which shapes in more complex ways, without any really noticeable change. Just as understanding of a language increases, likewise the understanding of a nation widens. What gains has the German language not made, to give but one example, since it has begun imitating Greek metre, and what developments have not taken place in the nation, not just in its learned part, but in its mass, even down to women and children, since the Greeks have really become the nation's reading matter in their true and unadulterated shape. Words fail to express how well-deserving of the German nation Klopstock has been with his first successful treatment of antique metre, and how much more so Voss, who may be said to have introduced classical antiquity into the German language. A more powerful and beneficial influence on a national culture can hardly be imagined in an already highly sophisticated time, and that influence is his alone. For he has invented the established form, even though it is still susceptible to improvement, in which alone, now and for as long as German is spoken, the ancients can be rendered in our language, and he could do so only because of his talent and the dogged perseverance of his character which indefatigably kept working at the same object — and whoever creates a true form may rest assured that his labour will last, whereas even a product of the highest genius remains without further consequence for progress along the same path if it is an isolated phenomenon and lacks such a form. If translation is to incorporate into the language and the spirit of a nation what it does not possess, or what it possesses in a different way, the first requirement is simple fidelity. This fidelity must be aimed at the real nature of the original, not at its incidentals, just as every good translation originates in simple and unpretentious love for the original and the research that love implies, and to which the translation must return. A necessary corollary to this conception is that a translation should have a certain foreign colouring over it, but the line beyond which this undeniably becomes a mistake can easily be drawn. Translation has reached its highest goals as long as what is felt is not strangeness, but merely what is strange; but where strangeness appears as such, and probably even obscures the strange, there the translator betrays that he is not up to his original. In this case the unprejudiced reader's feelings do not easily miss the dividing line. If one goes even beyond this, in fearful awe of the unwonted, and strives to avoid the strange itself, as we have heard it said that the translator should write the way the author of the original would have written in the language of the translator (a thought which has been formulated without reflection on the fact that no writer would have written the same thing in the same way in another language, exception made for science and physical objects) one destroys all translation and whatever advantages translation may bring to a language and a nation. For how else can it be explained that, even though all Greeks and Romans have been translated into French, and some have been translated very well in the French fashion, not the slightest shred of the spirit of antiquity has entered the nation with them, indeed that not even the national understanding of them (for we cannot speak of single scholars here) has increased in the least?

To come to my own work after these general observations: I have tried to approximate the simplicity and fidelity described above. At every rewriting I have tried to remove more of what was not contained in the text with the same simplicity. Inability to attain the peculiar beauty of the original all too easily entices one to lend it a strange glitter from which, on the whole, a deviant colouring and a different tone originate. I have tried to avoid obscurity and un-Germanness, but in the latter respect one should not make unjust requirements that might preclude higher advantages. A translation cannot and should not be a commentary. It should not contain obscurities originating in vacillating use of language and clumsy construction; but where the original only hints, without clearly expressing, where it allows itself metaphors whose meaning is hard to grasp, where it leaves out mediating ideas, there the translator would go wrong if he were to introduce, of his own accord, a clarity which disfigures the character of the text. The obscurity one often finds in the writings of the ancients, and which is especially present in the *Agamemnon*, originates in the brevity and the boldness with which thoughts, images, feelings, memories, suspicions are linked together as they originate in deeply felt emotions, with no regard for mediating sentences to connect them. The more you enter into the atmosphere of the poet, of his time, of the characters he puts on the stage, the more that obscurity vanishes and a high clarity takes its place. You must give a part of this attention to the translation too; you should not demand that what is noble, gigantic, and unusual in the original language should be easy and immediately intelligible in the translation. Yet ease and clarity always remain advantages that a translator gains with the utmost difficulty, and never through labour and rewriting; he owes them for the major part to a happy inspiration, and I know only too well to what extent my translation is deficient in this respect . . .

I have followed this edition [Gottfried Hermann's *Agamemnon*] as closely as possible. For I have always hated the eclectic manner in which translators often arbitrarily choose among the hundreds of variants in manuscripts and emendations made by critics, trusting to a feeling which, of necessity, often leads them astray. The edition of an ancient author is the reconstitution of a document, if not in its true and original form, at least as close as possible to the earliest accessible source. It must therefore be the product of one mind, the result of historical precision and conscientiousness, of the whole treasure of scholarship which underscores it, and preferably of a consistency which permeates it from beginning to end. On no account should what is called the esthetic sense be allowed to interfere (even though translators especially may believe they have a calling for it) if one does not want to impose ideas on the text which sooner or later give way to other ideas — the very worst that can befall an adapter of the ancients.

I have devoted the most meticulous care to the metrical part of my work, especially to the purity and exactness of the metre, since that is the basis of all other beauty, and I believe that no translator could possibly exaggerate in this. The rhythm, as it rules among Greek poets, and especially among the dramatists, to whom no metre is strange, is a world of its own, so to speak, even when it is separated from thought and from the music accompanied by melody. It represents the dark side of feeling and sentiment before it pours itself out in words, or when its sound has died away before it. The shape of all grace and nobility, the individuality of each character rests in it, evolves in free fulness, unites into ever new creations, is pure form, not weighed down by any matter, and reveals itself in tones, in other words in what grips the soul most deeply, because it is closest to the essence of inner perception. The Greeks are the only people we know of who were in possession of such a rhythm, and it is this fact which, in my opinion, characterizes and defines them to the highest extent. What we find of it in other nations is imperfect; what we and even (exeption made for a very few felicitous metres in their literature) the Romans possess is but an echo, both weak and uncouth. In judging languages and nations much too much attention has been paid to what I would call the dead elements, the outward diction; one always thinks everything is to be found in the spiritual. This is not the place to go into detail, but it has always seemed to me that it is precisely the manner in which letters are united into syllables in a language, and syllables into words, and the way these words in turn relate to each other in rhythm and tone, which describes or determines the intellectual, and to no small extent indeed the moral and political fate of nations. And in this the Greeks were blessed with the happiest fate that can befall a nation which wishes to rule through word and spirit, not power and action. Among modern languages only German seems to possess the advantage of being able to imitate this rhythm, and whoever combines a feeling for the dignity of the language with a sense of that rhythm will attempt to endow the language with more and more of this advantage. For it can be increased: like an instrument, a language must be played to the hilt; the ear of many who have been misled by the arbitrary behaviour of poets needs even more exercise, and the ear of those who do not read often must be especially trained in the less habitual metres. A translator, particularly of the ancient lyricists, often can win only by allowing himself certain liberties; few will follow him closely enough in the choric parts to examine whether he has used a syllable rightly or wrongly; indeed, if two possibilities are equally right many prefer, as Voss so very aptly pointed out in his time, a certain naturalness to the higher beauty of rhythm. But here a translator must exercise abnegation and self-discipline: in that way only will he walk a road on which he may hope to have more fortunate successors. For translations are definitely works which should examine, define, and influence the state of a language at a given point in time, as if measured against a timeless touchstone, and they must always be re-attempted as works designed to last. Moreover, the part of the nation which is unable to read them learns to know the ancients better by means of many translations than by means of one. They are as many images of the same spirit; for each renders the spirit he has been able to grasp and represent; the true spirit rests in the original text alone.

[From the "Einleitung" to *Aeschylos' Agamemnon metrisch übersetzt von Wilhelm von Humboldt* (1816) as reprinted in WvH, *Gesammelte Schriften,* 1. Abteilung, Bd. 8 (Berlin-Zehlendorf: Behr, 1909), 119-146. Reprinted in Störig, 71-96.]

August Wilhelm Schlegel, 1767-1845

Translating literature probably occupies a more central position in A. W. Schlegel's life than in that of his predecessors and successors. Only "translation provided Schlegel with the productive bridging of the gap between his unproductive poetic talent and his great critical ability . . ." (Huyssen, 74).

It is not merely a literary activity: "poetic translation, characterized by imperfect approximation and therefore to be continued indefinitely, stands to the original in a relationship of analogy similar to that of the poetry of the work itself which is, in its turn, analogous to the totality of the universe" (Huyssen, 94). To A. W. Schlegel and his brother Friedrich, translation is metaphor, conceptual category, as it was for Herder.

In his statements on literary translation A. W. Schlegel reasserts many points made by his predecessors and by his contemporaries, as well as contributing a number of insights of his own. The weightiest of these, in terms of the consequences it was to have for the theory and practice of literary translation in Germany during the following century, is his insistence that the form of the original should be kept in the translation. Form to him means, above all, metre. Yet he is inconsistent in this demand. He defends imitation in certain cases, apparently without realizing that this brings him very close to the French practice he — one is almost tempted to say ritually — denounces. His claim for the hexameter as a universal form can hardly be validated, and his statement that classical metres may work in a translation, but not in an original, appear to weaken somewhat the resolute identification he proclaims of poet and translator. The distinction he makes between ways of translating a work in which the writer reveals himself, as opposed to a work in which he does not, surfaces again, in a somewhat modified form, in the recent work of Katharina Reiss.

A. W. Schlegel also rejects any atomization of the work to be translated. Fidelity is to the whole, not to parts, and it is not be found in literalness, but in equivalence. His assertion that all acts of speaking and writing are, at bottom, acts of translation, is taken up again by Rosenzweig and by many contemporary theorists, both inside and outside of the German tradition. His idea that translations into German should make the German language into a kind of cosmopolitan centre for Europe and the world, first voiced by Goethe, is taken over by Schleiermacher and greatly expanded by him. Ironically, this idea has become a reality (or at the very least a near-reality) in our century, but the languages are English and Russian, not German.

Like Goethe, A. W. Schlegel draws attention to and produces translations of literature from "exotic languages". Ironically, again, these translations more or less force him to abandon, or at least to reconsider, claims other German theorists had been making or were making on behalf of the German language.

In his treatment of language itself A.W. Schlegel is even more cautious than Humboldt: the translator should not try to go beyond the boundaries of his own language. In some passages Schlegel's view of language even suggests the Whorfian "cryptotype", those elements of language which defy analysis and yet determine that language's real nature.

Finally, Schlegel's greatest insight has not yet been generally accepted, let alone realized, in the twentieth century, even though its validity is, to my mind, in no doubt. "A thought arises, the thinking of which requires some courage: the task of the critical scholar of literature is not just that of collecting and transmitting critical insight; rather he should − this seems to be the most important task Schlegel implies − test and prove his critical insight in scientifically precise translation. Recreation through translation and critical analysis of poetic works share a hermeneutic relationship, which is, for Schlegel, by no means a vicious circle but rather the basis of all historical insight. The union of translator and literary scholar, of recreative artist and universally educated savant, is valid even today as the ideal requirement, albeit only a few will be willing and able to strive after this ideal . . ." (Huyssen, 120). The fact that only a few are able, even though more than a few may be willing, goes a long way to explain why this capital insight of Schlegel's has failed to meet with general acceptance. Anyone can produce some kind of critical work; not everyone can express his critical understanding of a work of literature in a recreation which is both artistic in nature and scientifically valid.

TRANSLATIONS AIMED AT THE AUTHOR OR HIS WORK

I have tried to germanize as faithfully as possible, because everything carries weight in this poet [Dante], because in him there rules a conscientious precision in thought, even though he allows himself boundless liberties in language and expression. He was never willing to abandon even the tiniest part of what he had to say, which is why the constraints of metre so often forced him into distorted constructions, strange usage, and mutilated words. I thought I would have to keep the rhyme and, as much as possible, the form of the *terza rima* if I did not want to take the poet out of his element, so to speak. It is obvious that much had to be lost, in spite of all love and labour. I have not been afraid to use outlandish and semi-archaic expressions, nor to roughen language and metre; on the contrary: I have tried to render the nature of the original according to the impression it made on me. To try to smoothe it over or to embellish it would be to destroy it.

The way in which you translate poetry must be determined by whether you aim at the author or at his work. There are works − and this way of writing poetry is most particular to epochs of refined taste — which betray little of what the artist is as a human being. They allow us to judge his abilities, his talents only. For this type of work aims to give the pleasure of poetic perfection, and its value should be measured accordingly. Esthetic faults considered in isolation are of no interest. Why then should the translator not be allowed to spare his reader these faults, to smoothe over what is rough, to shed light on what is dark, to correct what has been wrongly represented — in short: to embellish. The more, however, the nature of the work is identical with the nature of its creator, the more it is an involuntary reproduction of his inner self, the more it becomes a duty to translate into the copy faithfully mistaken idiosyncracies, the wilfulness of his nature, and the shortcoming of (or false directions taken in) his education; these are of moral and psychological importance and often very intricately interwoven with the noblest qualities. We like to have the work of art in its perfection; the man we prefer to have as he is.

Numismatics is familiar with the concept of what is called noble rust (*aeruga nobilis*) as a sign of the authenticity of old coins. That rust on a copper coin is of more value to the expert than gold, and whoever might want to clean the coin would be taken for an ignorant outsider, at the very least. Counterfeiters have learned to improve on everything, except this stamp of the centuries. People, heroes, sages, and poets likewise have this noble rust. It is a sign of something amazingly important, namely that their greatness has not been the product of culture and cultivation; that, in an era of writings in manuscript, lack of training, and clumsiness, these people transcended all this by their own power. Only a former Frenchman could unfeelingly polish this away in descriptions or translations, merely so he might show the world a shining penny with all the more self-gratification. Who is to guarantee that the rust will not be coined again in the next coin?

[From August Wilhelm Schlegel, *Dante — Über die Göttliche Komödie* (1795), as printed in AWS, *Sämmtliche Werke* (ed. Ed. Böcking; Leipzig: Weidmannsche Buchhandlung, 1846).]

THE IMPACT OF TRANSLATION ON THE NATIVE TRADITION

More than thirty years ago a writer [Wieland] who, because of the fertility of his own mind, seemed least destined to become a translator, but who afterwards became a classic for us in this field as well, dared undertake for the first time the Herculean labour of translating most of Shakespeare into German. That labour was all the more herculean then, because there were fewer aids to the knowledge of the English language, and not much had been done to explain this often difficult and occasionally quite unintelligible poet — not even in England.

He was not immediately given the credit he deserved, and that is hardly surprising, because our theatres were still generally dominated by inspired imitations from the French, and even our best dramatic works were written completely with French models in mind. Who would then have dared to imagine that such pagan, unruly, barbaric plays which obscure rumor ascribed to a certain Englishman, a William Shakespeare, would ever have been allowed to be shown before our eyes? Lessing, that valiant enemy of prejudice, was the first to reveal French tragic wit in its nakedness, to praise Shakespeare's merit in an emphatic voice, and to remind the Germans that they possessed a translation of that great poet they could learn from for a long time — even though it had its defects — before they would need a new one.

To be sure he could not have foreseen what happened a few years later. The style of his own dramatic works, especially *Emilia Galotti*, helped arouse his fellow citizens' receptivity to Shakespeare. The publication of *Götz von Berlichingen* was, in combination with a few other circumstances, to create a whole new epoch in our theatres, for better and for worse. Not long before that only the Englishman had been praised with a glowing eloquence that would sweep his opponents away, even if it failed to convince them, and the truth was impressed upon us all that the whole caboodle of the rules of fashionable refinement simply could not be used as a yardstick for his creations. Only nine years after Wieland's translation had been published the need was felt, not for a reprint, but for a better germanization of all of Shakespeare's works. Since Wieland himself could not undertake this task, it fortunately fell to one of our most learned and most tasteful men of letters [Johann Joachim Eschenburg], whose sound knowledge of the language, uncommon ingenuity in explication, and assiduous care gave the translation what it had been lacking until then: overall completeness and precision of detail.

Even though the knowledge of English has spread widely in Germany, it very rarely attains the degree which is required if one is not to be continuously interrupted in one's pleasure, or even scared away from reading the poet. How few are there among those who can read him in his totality (that is to say, those passages excepted where the English themselves need a commentary because the words have become obsolete, the allusions unknown, or the texts corrupt) without interruption — how few are there who can feel and recognize, with a facility equal to that in their mother tongue, all the more refined beauty, the tender nuances of expression on which the harmony of a poetic representation rests? How few have mastered English pronunciation to the extent that they can read the poet aloud with the required emphasis and euphony. Yet all this greatly increases his impact, since poetry is obviously not a silent art. Readers of Shakespeare who have passed all the tests described above would not be adverse, for the sake of change, to rest now and again on their own soil in the shadow of his works, if those works could be transplanted without too great a loss of their beautiful leafwork. Would it therefore not be a very good thing if we had a translation? "But we have one already, and it is complete, and faithful, and good." So it is! We had to have that much to be able to wish for more. The desire for luxury follows the satisfaction of basic needs; now the best in this field is no longer good enough for us. If Shakespeare could and should only be translated into prose, then we ought to rest content with what has been achieved so far. But he is a poet, also in the sense in which one connects this word to the use of metre. If it were possible to recreate his work faithfully and yet at the same time poetically, to follow the letter of his meaning step by step and yet to catch part of the innumerable, indescribable marvels which lie not in the letter, but float above it like a breath of the spirit! It is worth a try.

[From August Wilhelm Schlegel, "Etwas über Wilhelm Shakespeare bei Gelegenheit Wilhelm Meisters" (1796), as printed in AWS, *Sämmtliche Werke* (1846).]

TRANSLATION AND PARAPHRASE'. THE FRENCH AND THE GERMAN MODEL

Frenchman: In [Klopstock's] *Gramatische Gespräche* [Dialogues on Grammar 1794] there is talk of a competition between languages — they would be classified according to their ability to translate. I must protest against this in the name of my own language. The criterion used is narrowly national in nature, because the Germans translate every literary Tom, Dick, and Harry. We either do not translate at all, or else we translate according to our own taste.

German: Which is to say, you paraphrase and you disguise.

Frenchman: We look on a foreign author as a stranger in our company, who has to dress and behave according to our customs, if he desires to please.

German: How narrow-minded of you to be pleased only by what is native.

Frenchman: Such is our nature and our education. Did the Greeks not hellenize everything as well?

German: In your case it goes back to a narrow-minded nature and a conventional education. In ours education is our nature.

Poetry: Be careful, German, don't exaggerate this positive trait. Unlimited education would be lack of character.

[From August Wilhelm Schlegel, "Der Wettstreit der Sprachen" (1798), as printed in AWS, *Sämmtliche Werke* (1846).]

THE PROBLEM OF ANNOTATIONS

In my opinion all annotations of individual passages should deal with objects, not words. Shakespeare is full of obscurities. Some of them are, if not intentional, at least original and in part characteristic: they arise from the compressed brevity, the bold liberties, the quick transition from one metaphor to another. Other obscurities have come into being by chance, in the course of time. Here the translator may, without weakening or paraphrase, make a mild turn in the direction of clarity and become a kind of practical commentator.

What is the aim of poetic recreation? I think it should provide those who have no access to the original with as pure and uninterrupted an appreciation of it as possible. The translator should therefore not resuscitate in the notes the difficulties he has already solved in the text. What use does the natural friend of poetry have for the laboriousness of textual criticism, variants, conjectures, emendations? The few learned readers who are able to compare will see at once which reading the translator has followed.

So we need explanations of objects only for the educated but unscholarly reader, either under the text, or with a reference at the end of the play. Who is going to check in Volume Three? A much more inportant need would be met by introductions of the kind I have attempted for *Romeo and Juliet*. In every one of Shakespeare's plays you are transported into a strange world, you have to acclimatize first. Nothing can shed more light on the poet's profound wit and the creative power of his genius than a comparison between the materials of his works, be they true or apocryphal stories, novellas, fairy tales, legends, etc., with what the poetic alchemist has made them into. Steevens and Malone [George Steevens and Edmund Malone, leading English Shakespeare scholars of the day] have conducted the search for Shakespeare's sources with great diligence, and they have unearthed much that was not known before. In this case one should, in my opinion, not save on paper, but give whole passages from [the sixteenth-century English historiographer Raphael] Holinshed, for example in a literal translation or in extracts, as an appendix to the historical plays. Sometimes the source is known, as in the case of the Roman plays, but few readers will be so familiar with Plutarch that they would immediately think of the biographer's hints which Shakespeare used and developed for his characterization. Often it would be as attractive as it is instructive (in the case of *King Lear*, for instance) not to be satisfied with the nearest source, but to go back to the most remote one available. What is the most remote source of these apocryphal stories? Ask about and see if any readers are able to answer that question. This type of research occupies a middle position between textual criticism and artistic judgment of the works as a whole; it may, of course, be instrumental in preparing the latter.

[From August Wilhelm Schlegel. "Schreiben an Herrn Reimer" (1828). as printed in AWS. *Sämmtliche Werke* (1846).]

METRICAL TRANSLATION

Poetic translation is a very difficult art. One could write a detailed essay on its principles, but not without devoting much attention to both grammatical and philological detail. Allow me to make just a fow short observations about it here, namely that this art was invented only a few years ago, if you leave a few exceptions out of consideration, and that this invention was reserved for German fidelity and perseverance. In the first period of their history, when they modelled their language (not without violence) after Greek forms, the Romans seem to have had, as far as we can judge from a few fragments, relatively faithful translations of Greek poems, though they were not altogether without roughness and clumsiness. In fact, everything started with translation in their case. Later, in what is called the Golden Age of their poetry, when it had evolved its own system of diction, it seems to have lost this ability more and more, and if people were not satisfied with free imitations, as was most often the case, the translations certainly lost character and became more mannered. Greek and Latin are, moreover, closely related; one could almost think of them as dialect and standard language, and in that case poetic recreation has been known to succeed to a very high degree without much of an effort, as for instance between the Spaniards and the Italians. Other nations have adopted a totally conventional phraseology in poetry and made it into an unbreakable rule, so that it is totally impossible to make a poetic translation of anything whatsoever into their language — French is an example and so is contemporary English, albeit to a lesser extent.

It is as if they want every foreigner among them to dress and behave according to the customs of the land, and that explains why they never really get to know a foreigner. If they torture themselves to the highest possible fidelity they do so in prose, which completely changes everything: they offer us the dead parts; the living breath has gone. Literalness is a long way from fidelity. Fidelity means that the same or similar impressions are produced, because these are the essence of the matter. That is why all translations of verse into prose ought to be condemned, because metre should not be just an external ornament (and it is not, in real poems) but it ranks among the original and essential prerequisites of poetry. Furthermore, since all metrical forms have a definite meaning, and their necessary character in a particular language may very well be demonstrated (for unity of form and essence is the aim of all art, and the more they interpenetrate and reflect each other, the higher is the perfection achieved), one of the first principles of the art of translation is that, for as far as the nature of a language allows, a poem should be recreated in the same metre. One is very much inclined to deviate from this, partly because it is very difficult, partly because one has grown fond of the practice as it has been up to this moment — two very good reasons why the greatest strictness should be proclaimed the law. It takes only despair that what has not yet been achieved will really happen, one day, to make the seemingly impossible come to pass. The German language has the great advantage that it is the only one, for the time being, in which the introduction of classical rhythmical metres has been successful to the point where they are generally accepted. The process began half a century ago, but only recently has it reached greater perfection, and much remains to be done. Many might doubt the value of these metres for their own production, even after the endeavours of great poets, or they might at least doubt the possible popularity of such poems. But its value has been proved beyond the shadow of a doubt for use in translations from the classics. In accentuated rhymed verse we have begun to cultivate Italian and Spanish forms, just as, in the past, we tended to imitate mostly the French, unfortunately, and later to some extent the English. If we follow this principle we can, therefore, more or less translate from the most important languages into ours. Yet I do not want this to be considered an advantageous feature which just happens to be present in the composition of our language. Others could also open themselves to a great variety of influences; all it takes is resolve and hard work.

This flexibility of ours finds its roots only in the fact that the German tries harder to participate in the movements and changes of the soul which correspond to those outside developments. The willingness in the German national character to translate itself into foreign ways of thinking and to abandon itself entirely to them finds expression in our language, which makes it the best translator and mediator for all others. Obviously the best translation can, when all is said and done, only be an approximation to an indefinable degree; if this were not so, one would have to carry out the same work with completely different tools and devices, which is, strictly speaking, impossible. Cervantes, who did not have much time for translation, because his was a very inventive mind, therefore compares poetic translations to the reverse side of Brussels tapestries: the shapes are still recognizable, but they are greatly disfigured by the threads that run together.

But, you will say, we have before us the works of a few of the greatest of the Greek dramatists which have come down to us, and we can compare them to the works of modern masters, if we please. Because the main features in drama are plot, characterization, pathos, etc., we shall therefore also find them without fail in the translations, and as a result we shall be able to judge them by secure standards, even if we do not know the original. I happen to have read lately what a journalist had to say about a translation of a few of Aeschylus' plays which had just been published: it is a good thing that there are translations, so that the excessively favourable opinion we have of the perfection of the old drama may be dampened a bit; we can now see their merits and their defects with our own eyes, we do not have to be told about them any more. For a journalist who does not know a word of Greek and who has not familiarized himself with classical antiquity in any other way, it may of course be a very good thing to have matters reduced to the yardstick of his own pettiness and to see them popularized in that way — so that he, too, can get a word in edgewise. We can rightly leave him to his arrogant and ridiculous ignorance. I must, however, remind friends of literature who want to acquire a more thorough knowledge of classical works of art that there is, for other European languages, not the faintest hope that the Greek tragedies will ever be translated into them in a satisfactory way — and that whatever has been done so far in German, which has in this case such a strong advantage over other languages, is still a long way from possible and definitely required perfection.

It is clear that even the most perfect translation can never equal the text in the original language which appears, in precisely that spot, at the highest point of its poetic development and in the most complex artistic forms. How then might anyone be so arrogant as to judge by bad translations, when even the text is only an incomplete extract from the work of art as it went forth vividly from the poet's soul to physical realization before a united nation?

[From August Wilhelm Schlegel, *Geschichte der klassischen Literatur* (1802), as printed in AWS, *Kritische Schriften und Briefe* (ed. Edgar Lohner; Stuttgart: Kohlhammer, 1962-1967), III (1964).]

TRANSLATION AS RECREATION

Yet what I have just praised as an advantage — diligence and skill in translating — is rejected by many as a mistaken habit. They say it originates in mental sluggishness and servility and leads to more of the same: it renders you incapable of personal creation and invention. As opposed to this it is easy to demonstrate that objective poetic translation is true writing, a new creation. Or if it is maintained that you should not translate at all, you would have to reply that the human mind hardly does anything else, that the sum total of its activity consists of just that. But it would carry us too far to develop this point here. Suffice it to say that higher artistic recreation has a nobler aim than the common craftsmanship of translation which exists only to remedy literary indigence. Its aim is nothing less than to combine the merits of all different nations, to think with them and feel with them, and so to create a cosmopolitan centre for mankind.

[From August Wilhelm Schlegel, *Geschichte der romantischen Literatur* (1803), as printed in AWS, *Kritische Schriften und Briefe* (ed. Edgar Lohner; Stuttgart: Kohlhammer, 1962-1967), IV (1965).]

IMITATION AND THE LIMITS OF A LANGUAGE

What I offer here is not a translation, but a free imitation. All literary translations are only imperfect approximations. The approximation can be rendered so imperfect by the inimitability and the unreachability of the original that it is better not to attempt it at all. Sanskrit appears to me to be such an unreachable and inimitable original, even if we abstract the quality and form of what is written in it. Sanskrit goes beyond everything the German language is capable of, and it does so to a much greater extent than Greek. Add to this the inexhaustible wealth of melodious and meaningful synonyms to denote objects, whereas we are always tied to the same expression. The grace will be lost in any case; and what is a literary form without grace but the letter of a law in which the spirit is not yet able to reveal itself by means of the unfettered exercise of its faculties.

Literal translations, in the sense of exact imitations of metrical form, could and can be of use for individual attempts somehow to give the reader an idea of the tone of the original, just as one allows a facsimile of a manuscript to be engraved in copper. I would not recommend this method for narrative poems which run to greater length.

I do not worry about the objection that I produce a strange travesty if I retell Sanskrit poetry in German hexameters. The hexameter is not a local, even less a chance invention: it is an immortal and universally valid form for all languages capable of incorporating it into themselves by virtue of their structure. Its main merit resides precisely in that it is, in its unity and change, the rhythmical expression of the spirit of the epic.

[From the "Vorerinnerungen" to August Wilhelm Schlegel's translations from the Sanskrit (1823), as printed in AWS, *Sämmtliche Werke* (1846).]

FIDELITY AND THE TRANSLATOR AS CREATOR OF LANGUAGE

Wieland has very rightly pointed out that fidelity or, to move away from the concept of literal accuracy which is so easily linked with that expression, truth, has to be the highest, indeed almost the only law for any translation of Homer. Artistic whim is allowed free play in the recreation of certain works, just as it was allowed free play in their first creation. A copy of this kind of work, no matter how different, has its value if it gives pleasure when considered by itself. Things become more dubious when what attracts us to the work is based in part on personal idiosyncracy, when the author has given an involuntary expression of his inner self in addition to what he wanted to represent. Nothing is separate in a single being: all characteristics partake of a continuous relationship, and when their inner composition cannot always be explained by means of concepts, you can feel (I am almost tempted to say see) it. Seemingly small changes are therefore often sufficient to show the whole in a false light. In a word: individuality cannot be divided into parts; it is hit or missed in its entirety.

The impression that a poetic representation should make depends, in the final analysis, only to a very limited extent on the meaning of words and locutions as they are perceived by the mind; it is through the living breath of speech, through a multitude of animate sounds that poetry — especially nature poetry, which precedes both science and the arts proper — lays claim to man's full understanding. One really has a sure and direct feeling for these often mixed strong and tender impulses only in one's mother tongue.

... a language must completely take the place of another, so that those common elements which cannot be regulated by means of general prescriptions can be observed in addition to its rules. All poetic translation, in which the heart of the matter is not just the meaning in general, but rather the most intricate connotations, remains therefore an imperfect approximation. No proof is needed that whatever licence an original poet is allowed should also be allowed in full to a poet who translates, because his situation is much less favourable. But it is just as certain that there are certain fixed limits for any language, whether they are caused by its original nature which still endures or by evolution since time immemorial. You cannot go beyond these limits without incurring the justified reproach that you are, in reality, not speaking a valid language, recognized as such, but rather a jargon of your own invention. No necessity can be adduced as a justification for this.

The problem of how far the right of the individual to contribute to the elaboration of language can be extended has recently been discussed. The history of languages proves that individual writers, especially poets, are able to exert an immeasurably large influence on this by means of their example. Much has, moreover, initially been condemned as corrupting a language which later entered into that language and proved itself to be, in reality, an ennobling factor. Proposals to introduce something into a language which is not yet available in it should therefore not be rejected without thorough consideration. Like all human institutions, language, that marvelous charter of our higher destiny, also strives after the better, and it is a real merit when the individual becomes an organ of this general desire through certain endeavours of his. There is only one indispensable condition: he should not demolish while he is engaged in the act of construction: the innovation which is being proposed should not be allowed to contradict what has been firmly established. If a language were merely something jumbled together, whether from similar or dissimilar components, a formless mass, one would be allowed to change it or add to it at will and every enrichment without exception would be a gain. But it is an ordered whole, or at least it claims to be growing into one, more and more; all its elements attract or reject each other according to the laws of kinship and similarity; general forms pervade it, bring matter to life and bind it together through their power. The simpler its laws, the more encompassing and coherent, the more perfect will be its organization. The more freedom establishes itself parallel to these laws, not opposed to them, the more a language is adapted to poetic use. Excess of positive law-giving which leaves little or no manœuvring space for the development of original dispositions is a great evil both in language and the state. If what is being said about the much praised plasticity of our language holds true, we do not suffer from this, at least not in comparison with other languages. We realize all the more easily that we are under the obligation not to impose anything on it which would be contrary to its nature, which could never melt into it until it became of the same nature. To be able to model oneself on a foreign nature, in the act of recreation, is true praise only when one has to assert one's independence at the same time and when one does, in fact, assert it.

The language-shaping artist's real element begins, therefore, where the grammarian's judicial functions cease. There are only a few cases in which the latter is allowed to interfere with the former's business, namely when he tries to censure a use of language which is obviously wrong and whimsical, one which obtains only in certain locutions and runs counter to the general analogy. He always does so at his own risk. Every positive law of language — and language itself — is a matter of general consensus anyway, if not in its origin, then at least in its developed form, and only that same power which laid down the law can revoke it again. The fact that one often fails to observe an inner necessity in this does not in the least detract from the status of language use. If you were to operate only with the principles of philosophical grammar, without any help from the individual, or even the whimsical, you could invent a kind of logical code notation, but never a living language. What has been commonly and irrevocably decided on remains so, even if you were able to show that chance had played a large part in it. You must, futhermore, beware of confusing characteristic idiosyncrasies with chance events. A law which you would be inclined to think of as one of the tyrannical tricks of much maligned common usage, if you take it on its own, often acquires a high degree of appropriateness and even a kind of individual necessity, which can be felt rather than represented, when it is considered in the context of the components and the whole construction of the language promulgating it.

[From August Wilhelm Schlegel, "Homers Werke von Johann Heinrich Voss" (1796), as printed in AWS. *Sämmtliche Werke* (1846).]

Friedrich Schlegel, 1772-1829

Friedrich Schlegel most radically conceives of translation as a category of thought rather than an activity connected with language or literature only. Indeed just as translation is a metaphor to him, so is poetry. He applies both terms, as well as critical terms taken from the study of literature, such as commentary, or idyll, to human activities other than those normally circumscribed by literature. Poetry is a metaphor for the world as a whole; translation becomes, therefore, the poetry of poetry.

Friedrich Schlegel insists, on a more practical level, that the translator should not only be familiar with the language he translates from, but also with the literature written in that language. His own familiar knowledge of classical literature, which he regarded as a completed, "organic" cycle of literature which could be projected on the modern literatures, gave an evolutionary dimension to his thinking on literature and translation. Literature is enriched by new forms, and these new forms are introduced by translators as well as by original writers. In fact, the forms that writers introduce in the translations they make sometimes outlive the original work they produce.

Friedrich Schlegel describes translation as both an art and a science, but his own propensity towards the mystical, the speculative, the unsystematic make a "scientific" reception of his insights unnecessarily difficult. The distinction he makes between medial and radical translation is reminiscent of the distinction made by his brother, with whom he also shares the conviction that criticism and the study of writers are peripheral activities in literary scholarship, whereas translation is a popular task.

The short epigrammatic notes in which most of Friedrich Schlegel's thoughts on translation are expressed reflect his conviction that the truth can never fully be reached. A succession of fragments is a succession of approximations — not unlike a succession of translations.

MAXIMS ON TRANSLATION AND TRANSLATORS

A good translator must literally be able to make, to construe all things literary.

All artists who do not improve on their art, but merely transplant what is alien into their homeland, are, properly speaking, translators.

You can also translate whole genres; the restoration of old forms is a poetic translation. (Parody is a witty translation.) Philosophy could be called a combinatory translation. Concept of metaphorical translations. Transcendental translations are concerned only with the spirit. Natural, empirical translations and artificial, methodical translations. [Wilhelmus] Wilhelm [a prominent theologian and Bible interpreter] the first philosophical translator. Klopstock's transplantation of old metrical systems a mythical translation. Translation is also very much a matter of instinct and purpose.

The real nature of the novella is the art of telling a story well, just as the real nature of translation from the classics is the art of describing, delineating.

[From Friedrich Schlegel, *Literary Notebooks, 1797-1804* (ed. Hans Eichner; London: Athlone Press, 1957).]

The best is what gets lost in your run-of-the-mill good or excellent translation.

Notes are philological epigrams, translations philological mimes, many commentaries for which the text is only the starting point or the not-I are philological idylls.

[From Friedrich Schlegel, "Kritische Fragmente", as printed in FS, *Kritische Schriften* (ed. Wolf-dietrich Rasch; München: Hanser, 1956).]

Many musical compositions are merely translations of poetry into the language of music.

To be able to translate to perfection from ancient into modern literature, the translator should know modern literature well enough to write it, and at the same time he should understand ancient literature well enough to recreate it, not just to imitate it.

The important point in connection with the problem of the possibility of translating classical writers is whether a faithful translation into the purest German is not somehow still Greek. One gets that suspicion from the impression translations make on the layman, who is most qualified and able to judge.

[From Friedrich Schlegel, "Athenäums-fragmente", as printed in FS, *Kritische Schriften* (München: Hanser, 1956).]

TRANSLATION AND THE INTRODUCTION OF NEW GENRES AND FORMS

Andrea: Superficial abstractions and arguments, a false understanding of antiquity, and mediocre talent produced in France a comprehensive and coherent system of false literature based on an equally mistaken theory of literature; and from there this feeble theory of so-called good taste spread to almost all European countries. The French and the English now constructed their respective Golden Ages and carefully elected their number of classics as worthy representatives of their nations to the Pantheon of Glory from among writers who ought not to be mentioned in a history of art.

Yet even here a tradition of going back to nature and antiquity managed to survive, and this spark set the Germans alight, after they had slowly assimilated their examples. Winckelmann taught them to look on antiquity as a whole and gave the first example of the way an art form should be rooted in the history of its formation. Goethe's universality provided them with a mild reflection of the literature of almost all times and all nations, an inexhaustibly instructive array of works, studies, sketches, fragments, attempts in every genre and in the most varied forms. With a few bold steps philosophy reached the point where it could understand itself as well as the human spirit in the depths of which it had to discover the primeval source of fantasy and the ideal of beauty. Thus it had to give clear acknowledgment to literature, whose essence it had not suspected until that time. Literature and philosophy, man's highest powers, which in the past worked separately, each in its own field, even in Athens at the time of its highest flowering, now reach out and grasp each other, to shape and invigorate each other in eternal reciprocity. The translation of poets and the recreation of their rhythms has become an art and criticism has become a science; old mistakes have been abolished and new perspectives opened in the knowledge of antiquity and the entire history of literature which reveals itself in it.

The Germans now only have to continue to use these methods, to follow the example set by Goethe, by tracing artistic forms everywhere back to their sources. In doing so they will be able to bring them back to life or to mix them; they likewise have to go back to the sources of their own language and literature and liberate the old power, the high spirit which has been slumbering until now, neglected in the documents of ancestral times from the *Nibelungenlied* to Fleming and Weckherlin [Paul Fleming and Georg Rudolph Weckherlin, two leading poets of the German seventeenth century]. Thus literature, which has not been shaped with such originality and fashioned to such perfection in any modern nation, literature, which was first a saga of heroes, then a game of knights, and finally a craft of burghers, will, in that same nation, become and remain a full science practiced by true scholars and an excellent art practiced by inventive writers.

Antonio: We also have examples among us, and very close to us, of masters who, perhaps without knowing it or even wanting to, paved the way for their successors. When Voss's own poems have long since vanished from the succession of things, his merits as a translator and linguistic virtuoso who made a new field arable with untold power and perseverance will shine all the more brightly the more his provisional works are superseded by better successors, because people will realize that these have been made possible only by his works.

[From Friedrich Schlegel, "Gespräch über die Poesie" (1800), as printed in FS, *Kritische Schriften* (München: Hanser, 1956).]

TRANSLATION AS A CATEGORY OF THOUGHT

Translation is really linguistic creation. Only the translator is an artist who works in language.

Translations are *mythical, physical (technical),* or *historical.*

Logic, the criticism of philosophy, would be a descriptive translation or a translative description. If you could write such a description of the universe, it would be a purely philosophical work — or would it not rather turn out to be a *Principles of Religion?* It would be a central text, no longer an isolated epic piece of writing that would be neither wholly poetic nor wholly philosophical. Bible in the real sense, Holy Writ.

All translation is poetic; even the very work on its own is poetic.

Translation is obviously philological in nature, as descriptions are; they both belong to art but also to science. All translation is transplantation or metamorphosis or both. An essay must have form; it is connected to a social dimension and a striving after universality (the Romans were the first translators). Every real translation must be rejuvenation.

Every history which does not refer to the chronology of the Spirit, the geography of the universe, the translation of mankind, is just an essay. Nearly all historical works which are not documents are diasceuastic translations.

An original is a translation square.

Just as description is the perfect work of criticism, just so translation is the perfect work of the human sciences and the highest sciences are chronology of the spirit and topography of the inner man (this is still almost in its Homeric childhood, everywhere is still Africa). It is the essence of the highest philology or criticism. The three elements are needed to produce a work: you have to translate your ideal, sketch out a blueprint of it, and then write a description. Literature is, therefore (taken in the practical sense as the art of composing the work), the highest philology.

Historical works should be translated medially; philosophical and poetic works should always be translated radically.

Just as there is a geography and a description of the universe, there should also be a translation of it.

For both translation and description much may be learnt from the copying painters do, the way musicians compose, and the diasceuastic declamation of actors. The author should always be a bookseller and a librarian as well.

A translation is a work of art which originates in the intellect; it refers to the concept of the dialectic. The imperative of translation must rest on the postulate of the unity of languages. All translations should at least be capable of being studies. "All translations up to now are essays only."

The forms of peripheral literature are, really: study, description, fragment, and perhaps rhapsody. Translation and representation are the popular forms of poetry.

Everything said about poetry except translations and annals always remains mysticism and it should therefore only be scattered about in brochures.

Descriptions are merely a form of translation, just like *explanations.*

Should a translation of Aristotle be of value for the shaping of pure prose? Should practical man be educated to pure prose or to historical prose?

The definition of man as a kind of translation is definitely valid.

Ethics and the *theory of method* also have to be *translated* into speculative philosophy, just as physics has to be translated into highest abstraction.

Philosophy is not a source, not a way of finding truth, rather it is an invaluable way of maintaining, purifying, and linking, by means of which truth is established in an *almost mystical manner* — it is also merely a kind of translation and a dressing up of truth, and so is literature.

[From Friedrich Schlegel, "Philosophische Fragmente" (1796), as printed in FS, *Werke* (Kritische Ausgabe; ed. Ernst Behler; München: Schöningh, 1958 ff.), XVIII (1963).]

CRITICISM OF THE TRADITION

The particular characteristics of language, the fine nuances by means of which one can, for instance, distinguish between several parts in Homer and conclude that there must have been different authors, are inevitably lost in the most faithful, most painstaking translations (those of Voss, for example) to the extent that there is no great difference, from the linguistic point of view, between Voss's translations of Homer, Hesiod, Theocritus, Virgil, and Ovid, who are very different from each other in the original, even though we may rightly require this of a faithful translation. We may therefore justly say that

Voss's translations do not offer a faithful image of Homeric poetry in its original form. The romantic poets of the Middle Ages came much closer to their goal by merely keeping the material which is romantic in the highest degree and to which Homer himself might have given a romantic form under other circumstances and in a language of a different shape: he might even have used rhyme.

[From Friedrich Schlegel, *Über das Studium der griechischen Poesie* (1797), as printed in FS, *Werke* (Kritische Ausgabe, ed. Ernst Behler: München: Schöningh, 1958 ff.).]

Novalis, 1772-1801

Translation is a metaphor and a category of thought for Novalis as well. But this metaphor has an eminently practical function: "because it is itself translation, poetry effects the *trans*-lation of mankind into the Golden Age and in doing so achieves the salvation of man and the fulfilment of the chiliastic-eschatological expectations Novalis had for the future" (Huyssen, 133). On a somewhat less lofty level, translation is no longer an approximation of the original, but rather its ideal. Both translation and original strive towards the ideal, but translation appears to be closer to it.

THREE KINDS OF TRANSLATION

A translation can be either grammatical, transforming, or mythical. Mythical translations are translations in the highest style. They represent the pure, completed nature of the individual work of art. They do not give us the real work of art, but its ideal. There is, I think, no model of them extant as yet. One does, however, find bright vestiges thereof in the spirit of many critical essays and descriptions of works of art. They require a mind in which the interpenetration of poetic and philosophical spirit is complete. Greek mythology is, in part, such a translation of a national religion. The modern Madonna is also such a myth.

Grammatical translations are translations in the ordinary sense. They require enormous erudition, but discursive abilities only.

Transforming translations require the highest poetic spirit, if they are to be authentic. They easily lapse into mere travesties, such as Bürger's iambic Homer, Pope's Homer, and all French translations. The true translator of this type must indeed be an artist himself; he must be able to render the idea of the whole in this manner or that, at will. He must be the poet's poet and therefore he must be able to let him speak both according to the poet's idea and to his own. A similar relationship exists between every individual human being and the genius of mankind.

All things can be translated according to these three methods, not just books.

[From Novalis, "Blüthenstaub", in *Athenäum* (1798), as reprinted (1960), 88-89. Reprinted in Störig, 33.]

TRANSLATION AS ORIGINAL WORK

Whoever reviewed your [A. W. Schlegel's] Shakespeare means well. But his review is most definitely not literature. What could not have been said about your Shakespeare, especially if measured against the Whole? It is among translations what *Wilhelm Meister* is among novels. Is there anything like it as yet? We Germans have been translating for a long time, and the desire to translate appears to be a national characteristic, since there is hardly a German writer of importance who has not translated, and who does not take as much pride in his translations as he does in his original works; and yet there seems to be nothing we know less about than — translation. With us it could become a science and an art. Your Shakespeare is an excellent canon for the scientific observer. Except for the Romans we are the only nation which has felt the urge to translate so irrepressibly and whose culture owes so immeasurably much to translation. Hence the many analogies between our literary culture and that of the later Romans. This urge is an indication of the very noble, original nature of the German people. Germans are essentially cosmopolitan, and at the same time strongly individualistic. For us alone translation has meant extension. Poetic morality, the sacrifice of one's inclinations, is required to undertake a real translation. One translates out of true love for the beautiful and for the literature of the nation. To translate is to produce literature, just as the writing of one's own works is — and it is more difficult, more rare.

In the end all literature is translation.

[From a letter to A. W. Schlegel, as printed in Novalis, *Werke und Briefe* (ed. Alfred Kelletat; München: Winkler, 1968).]

Friedrich Schleiermacher, 1768-1834

Schleiermacher's essay on the different methods of translating is the most triumphalistic formulation of a number of topics which have been part of the German tradition since Luther. Schleiermacher distinguishes between the activities of the translator and the interpreter, whereas Luther used the word interpreter indiscriminately for both. By firmly establishing the distinction Schleiermacher no doubt wanted to heighten the translator's prestige. He is close to Luther in requesting "translations in which the hallowed original will be, so to speak, 'translucent', in which every part of the text, even the smallest and most insignificant, is sacrosanct and must be preserved. This sanctitiy of the word which rests in the spiritual text is now extended to the inspired poetic word. This opinion is also accepted by modern translators and theorists of translation with a theological background, especially Jewish translation theorists (Buber, Rosenzweig, Benjamin) ..." (Senger, 87). These theorists, and many others have, unfortunately, also inherited much of Schleiermacher's style, which tends to render their writings, as it does his, needlessly convoluted and obscure.

Schleiermacher's attack on the paraphrasts is, in fact, aimed at Gottsched and his followers and at the Leibnizian theories of language they accepted. Yet he sides with Gottsched in condemning the act of writing serious creative work in a language other than one's mother tongue as unethical. Schleiermacher works out in detail Goethe's maxim on the reader-author-translator relationship, at the same time incorporating Goethe's three kinds of translation into his essay. The opposition between writings in which the author is visible and those in which he is not, first pointed out by A. W. Schlegel, also resurfaces here.

As Huyssen indicates, "At the beginning of his essay Schleiermacher manages to make statements which are eminently valid, by highlighting that midpoint at which the reader and the author of a work should meet. But towards the end of his investigations he succumbs to an excessively sharp polarization of the two antagonistic methods, fascinated as he is by his idea of the language of translation. In doing so he opens up a superfluous weakness to criticism and robs his theory of a fascinating impact, the more so since his idea of the language of translation is called into question, to say the least, by the kind of German he used in his translation of Plato ..." (Huyssen, 65). Indeed, Schleiermacher's argumentation is rather far-fetched in places. His positive eulogy of translationese is hard to accept, and the distinction he makes between bonded and free language has turned out to be spurious. The prospect of the application of his method on a massive scale, so that all different shades of foreignness might be represented in the translationese, is moreover clearly utopian.

To us the very standard Schleiermacher proposes seems mistaken, but we must keep in mind that this is due to the fact that his ideal reader (we first met him in Breitinger), who knows foreign languages quite well but is nevertheless conscious of the differences between them and his mother tongue, has become a vanishing breed in an age which gravitates increasingly towards the mono-lingual. Consequently, his requirement that the translation should "give the feel" of the source language must also strike us increasingly as odd.

He does, not seem to realize, moreover, that his concept of German transla-tionese as the repository of world literature (a concept taken over from A. W. Schlegel), which would be accessible to all those who have learnt German, appears to invalidate the claim that the foreignness of the source language should be visible in the translationese: the result would merely turn out to be a kind of foreignness twice removed. Schleiermacher's insistence on rendering "foreignness" lures him beyond the sensible limits which both Humboldt and A. W. Schlegel had set for this kind of endeavour, and forces him towards the type of atomization of the source text which will be taken up again by Scho-penhauer and is to dominate much of the theory and practice of literary translation during the remainder of the nineteenth century and the first dec-ades of the twentieth.

On the positive side Schleiermacher explicitates the insight first voiced by Herder, and reaffirmed by A. W. Schlegel, that translation is not just something which happens between languages. It also takes place inside languages, be-tween individuals and social classes. Schleiermacher is also quite right in stating that translations should not be made at the whim of the prospective translator (think of the interminable flow of Heine translations into English), but only when there is a genuine need for them. In saying this he is not too far removed from Goethe's concept of the clearing-house.

Ironically, what Schleiermacher calls "imitation" would correspond most closely to the ideal of literary translation accepted by the consensus of theorists nowadays. One might ask two questions in this connection: in how far does this concept fail to bring author and reader together, and in how far does Schleiermacher's own translationese keep them apart?

Finally, some of Schleiermacher's formulations anticipate Wittgenstein's notion of the language game. The two theorists even use similar arguments against the possibility of transcending it, while both remain blind to the fact that it is being transcended all the time.

ON THE DIFFERENT METHODS OF TRANSLATING

The fact that speech is translated from one language into another confronts us everywhere, under a wide variety of guises. On the one hand this allows people to establish contact who were originally as far apart from each other as the length of the earth's diameter; products of another language that has been dead for many centuries may be incorporated into a language. On the other hand we do not even have to go outside the domain of one language to encounter the same phenomenon. For not only are the dialects spoken by different tribes belonging to the same nation, and the different stages of the same language or dialect in different centuries, different languages in the strict sense of the word, not infrequently requiring a complete translation between them; moreover even contemporaries who are not separated by dialects, but merely belong to different classes which are not often linked through social intercourse and are far apart in education, often can understand each other only by means of a similar mediation. Are we indeed not often required to translate the speech of another for ourselves, even if he is totally our equal but possesses a different frame of mind or feeling? For when we feel that the same words would, in our mouth, have a totally different sense, or at least a stronger weight here and a weaker impact there than in his, and that, if we wanted to express the same things he meant, we would make use of totally different words and locutions, according to our nature – it seems, if we define this feeling more closely, and as it becomes a thought for us, that we translate. Indeed, we must sometimes even translate our own words after a while, when we want to make them really our own again. And this ability is not only exercised to transplant into foreign soil what a language has produced in the field of scholarship and the arts of speech and to enlarge the radius within which these products of the mind can operate by doing so; it is also exercised in the domain of trade between different nations and in the diplomatic commerce individual governments have with each other, in which each is accustomed to talking to the other in its own language only, if they want to ensure that they are treated on a basis of strict equality without having to make use of a dead language.

We do not, of course, wish to incorporate everything that lies within this wide radius into our present observations. The necessity to translate even inside one's own language and dialect, which is more or less an immediate need of the emotions, is too much a thing of the moment in its impact to need any guidance other than that given by the emotions; and if rules were to be promulgated about this, they could only be the rules following which man keeps a purely moral mood for himself, so that his receptivity for the less congenial remains open as well. If we exclude this and concern ourselves for the time being with translation from a foreign language into ours, we shall be able to distinguish two different fields here as well – not totally distinct of course, this is very rarely the case, but separated by boundaries which overlap, and yet separated clearly enough if one keeps their goals in sight. The interpreter plies his trade in the field of commerce; the translator proper operates mainly in the fields of art and scholarship. Those who find this definition arbitrary, because interpreting is usually taken to mean what is done orally and translating what is written, will, I am sure, forgive me for using them, for they are very conveniently tailored to fit the present need, the more so since the two definitions are by no means far removed from each other. Writing is appropriate to the fields of art and scholarship, because writing alone gives their works endurance, and to interpret scholarly or artistic products by word of mouth would be as useless as it seems to be impossible. For commerce, on the other hand, writing is but a mechanical means; oral bargaining is the original form here, and all written interpreting should really be considered the notation of oral interpreting.

Two other fields are joined to this one, very closely as regards their nature and spirit, yet because of the great multiplicity of objects belonging to them they already make a transition, one to the field of art, the other to that of scholarship. For each transaction which includes interpreting is a fact the development of which is perceived in two different languages. But the translation of writings which are purely narrative or descriptive in nature, which also merely translates the development, already described, of a fact into another language, can still include much of the interpreter's trade. The less the author himself appears in the original, the more he has merely acted as the perceiving organ of an object, and the more he has adhered to the order of space and time, the more the translation depends upon simple interpreting. Thus the translator of newspaper articles and the common literature of travel is, at first, in close proximity to the interpreter, and he risks becoming ridiculous when his work makes greater claims and he wants to be recognized as an artist. Alternatively, the more the author's particular way of seeing and shaping has been dominant in the representation, the more he has followed some freely chosen order, or an order defined by his impression, the more his work is a part of the higher field of art — and the translator, too, must then bring other powers and abilities to bear on his work and be familiar with his author and his author's language in another way than the interpreter is. On the other hand every transaction which involves interpreting is the drawing up of a specific case according to certain legal obligations; the translation is made only for participants who are sufficiently familiar with these obligations, and the way these obligations are expressed in the two languages is well defined, either by law or by custom and mutual explanation. But the situation is different, even though formally it may be very similar to what we have just referred to, in the case of transactions by means of which new legal obligations are established. The less these can be subsumed as particular cases under a sufficiently known general rule, the more scholarly knowledge and circumspection are required in formulating them, and the more scholarly knowledge of fact and language the translator will need for his trade. On this double scale, therefore, the translator rises more and more above the interpreter, until he reaches his proper field, namely those mental products of scholarship and art in which the free idiosyncratic combinatory powers of the author and the spirit of the language which is the repository of a system of observations and shades of moods are everything, in which the object no longer dominates in any way, but is dominated by thoughts and emotions, in which, indeed, the object has become object only through speech and is present only in conjunction with speech.

What is the basis of this important distinction? Everyone perceives it even in borderline cases, but it strikes the eye most strongly at the outer poles. In the life of commerce one is, for the most part, faced with obvious objects, or at least with objects defined with the greatest possible precision; all transactions have an arithmetical or a mathematical character, so to speak, and number and measure help out everywhere; and even in the case of those objects which, as the ancients were wont to say, subsume the more and the less into themselves and are referred to by means of a gradation of words, which weigh now more, now less in common life, because their essence is not defined, an established usage of individual words soon arises through law and custom. When, therefore, the speaker does not intentionally construct hidden indeterminacies, or make a mistake in order to deceive or because he is not paying attention, he can be understood by everyone who knows the language and the field, and at the most only unimportant differences appear in the use of language. Even so there are rarely any doubts that cannot be immediately dispelled as to which expression in one language corresponds to an expression in another. Translating in this field is, therefore, almost a mechanical activity which anyone can perform who has a fair to middling knowledge of both languages, and in which there is little distinction between better and worse, as long as the obviously wrong is avoided. But when the products of art and scholarship have to be transplanted from one language to another, two considerations appear which completely change the relationship. For if, in the case of two languages, one word in one language exactly corresponded to one word in the other, if it expressed the same concept to the same extent, if their declensions represented the same relationships and the ways in which they connect sentences matched, so that these languages were indeed different to the ear only — then all translation in the field of art and scholarship would be as mechanical as it is in the field of commerce, in so far as it communicated only the contents of a spoken or written text, and it could be said of every translation that except for the effects produced by sound and melody, it puts the foreign reader in the same relationship to the author and his work as the native reader. But the case with all languages which are not so closely related that they can almost be considered different dialects only is precisely the opposite, and the farther they are apart in time and genealogical descent, the less a word in one language corresponds completely to a word in another or a declension in one language comprehends exactly the same multiplicity of relationships as another in a different language. Since this irrationality, if I may call it that, pervades all elements of two languages, it should obviously also make an impact on the domain of social intercourse. Yet it clearly exerts much less pressure there, and it has as good as no influence. All words denoting objects and actions which may be of importance have been verified, so to speak, and even if empty, overcautious inventiveness might still wish to guard against a possible unequal value of words, the subject matter itself immediately restores the balance. Matters are completely different in the domains of art and scholarship and wherever thought, which is one with the word, not the thing of which the word is only a possibly arbitrary but fixed sign, dominates to a greater extent. For how endlessly difficult and complex the problem becomes here! What precise knowledge and what mastery of both languages it presupposes! And how often the most expert and best versed in languages, starting from a shared conviction that an equivalent expression cannot be found, differ significantly when they want to show which expression is the closest approximation. This holds true both of the most vivid pictorial expressions in poetic works and of the most abstract terms denoting the innermost and most general components of the highest scholarship.

The second consideration which changes true translation into an activity that is radically different from mere interpreting is the following: whenever the word is not completely bound by obvious objects or external facts it merely has to express, wherever the speaker is thinking more or less independently, and therefore wants to express himself, he stands in a double relationship to language, and what he says will be understood correctly only in so far as that relationship is perceived correctly. On the one hand every man is in the power of the language he speaks, and all his thinking is a product thereof. He cannot think anything with great precision which would lie outside the limits of language; the shape of his concepts, the nature and the limits of the way in which they can be connected, is prescribed for him by the language in which he is born and educated — intellect and imagination are bound by it. Yet on the other hand every freely thinking, mentally self-employed human being shapes his own language. For in what other way — except precisely by means of these influences — would it have developed and grown from its first raw state to its more perfect elaboration in scholarship and art? In this sense, therefore, it is the living power of the individual which creates new forms by means of the plastic material of language, at first only for the immediate purpose of communicating a passing consciousness; yet now more, now less of it remains behind in the language, is taken up by others, and reaches out, a shaping force. It might even be said that a person deserves to be heard beyond his immediate environment only to the extent to which he influences language. Any verbal text soon dies away of necessity if it can be reproduced by a thousand organs in a form which is always the same; only that text can and may endure longer which constitutes a new element in the life of a language itself. Therefore each free and higher speech needs to be understood twice, once out of the spirit of the language of whose elements it is composed, as a living representation bound and defined by that spirit and conceived out of it in the speaker, and once out of the speaker's emotions, as his action, as produced and explicable only out of his own being. Indeed, any speech of this kind is only understood, in the higher sense of the word, when these two relationships have been perceived together and in their true relation to each other, so that we know which of the two dominates on the whole or in individual parts. We understand the spoken word as an act of the speaker only when we feel at the same time where and how the power of language has taken hold of him, where in its current the lightning of thought has uncoiled, snake-like, where and how the roving imagination has been held firm in its forms. We understand the spoken word as a product of language and as an expression of its spirit only when we feel that only a Greek, for instance, could think and speak in that way, that only this particular language could operate in a human mind this way, and when we feel at the same time that only this man could think and speak in the Greek fashion in this way, that only he could seize and shape the language in this manner, that only his living possession of the riches of language reveals itself like this, an alert sense for measure and euphony which belongs to him alone, a power of thinking and shaping which is peculiarly his. If understanding in this field is difficult, even in the same language, and presupposes a deep and precise penetration into the spirit of the language and the author's proper nature, how much more will it not be a high art when one speaks of the products of a distant and foreign language! Whoever has mastered this art of understanding through the most diligent cultivation of a language, through precise knowledge of the whole historical life of a nation and through the living representation of single works and their authors, he and he alone may wish to lay open the same understanding of the masterpieces of art and scholarship to his contemporaries and compatriots. But the risks accumulate when he prepares himself for his task, when he wishes to define his goals more accurately and he surveys the means at his disposal. Should he resolve to bring two people who are so fully separated from each other as the man who speaks his own language, but not that of the author, and the author himself — to bring these two into a relationship so immediate as the one which exists between an author and his original reader? Or does he merely want to lay open for his readers the same understanding and the same pleasure he himself enjoys, with the traces of hardship it carries and the feeling of the strange which remains mixed into it. How can he achieve the second, let alone the first, with the means at his disposal? If his readers are to understand, they must perceive the spirit of the language which was the author's own and be able to see his peculiar way of thinking and feeling, and to realize these two aims the translator can offer them nothing but his own language, which at no point fully corresponds to the other, and his own person, whose understanding of his author is now more, now less clear, and whose admiration and approval of him is now greater, now less. Does not translation, considered in this way, seem a foolish enterprise? That is why people, in despair at not reaching this goal, or, if you prefer, before they had reached the stage at which all this could be clearly thought out, discovered two other methods of becoming acquainted with works in foreign languages, not with a view to gathering their real artistic or linguistic sense, but rather to fill a need and to contemplate spiritual art; in these methods some of these difficulties are forcibly removed, others slyly circumvented, but the concept of translation adduced here is completely abandoned.

These two methods are paraphrase and imitation. Paraphrase strives to conquer the irrationality of languages, but only in a mechanical way. It says: even if I do not find a word in my language which corresponds to a word in the original language, I still want to try to penetrate its value by adding both restrictive and expansive definitions. Thus it laboriously works itself through to an accumulation of empty particulars, caught between a troublesome too much and a painful too little. In this way it may possibly succeed in rendering the content with limited precision, but it totally abandons the impression made by the original, for the living speech has been killed irrevocably, since everybody feels that it cannot originally have proceeded — as it is — from the feelings of a human being. The paraphrast treats the elements of the two languages as if they were mathematical signs which may be reduced to the same value by means of addition and subtraction, and neither the spirit of the language transformed nor that of the original language are given the opportunity to reveal themselves in this method. If, moreover, the paraphrase attempts to mark psychologically the traces of the conjunction of thoughts — where they are unclear and strive to lose themselves — by means of the interjected sentences which it inserts as so many landmarks, in this way it also tries to take the place of a commentary in the case of difficult compositions, and it can, therefore, even less be reduced to the concept of translation. Imitation, on the other hand, submits to the irrationality of languages; it grants that one cannot render a copy — which would correspond precisely to the original in all its parts — of a verbal artefact in another language, and that, given the difference between languages, with which so many other differences are connected, there is no option but to produce an imitation, a whole which is composed of parts obviously different from the parts of the original, but which would yet in its effects come as close to that whole as the difference in material allows. Such an imitation is now no longer that work itself, and in no way should the spirit of the original language be represented in it and be active in it; on the contrary, many things are exchanged for the foreignness that spirit has produced: a work of this kind should merely be, as much as possible, and as far as the difference in language, morals, education allows, the same thing for its readers as what the original was for its own — to save the analogy of impression one abandons the identity of the work. The imitator, therefore, does not attempt to bring the two parties — the writer and the reader of the imitation — together, because he does not think a direct relationship between them is possible; he merely wants to produce on the reader an impression similar to that received from the original by its contemporaries who spoke the same language. Paraphrase is more current in the domain of scholarship, imitation in that of art; and just as everyone confesses that a work of art loses its tone, its brilliance, its whole artistic essence in paraphrase, just so no one has as yet undertaken the foolish task of producing an imitation of a scholarly masterpiece which treats its content freely. Both methods fail, however, to satisfy the person who, permeated by the value of a foreign masterpiece, wishes to extend its operational radius to those who speak his language and keeps the stricter concept of translation in mind. Neither can therefore be considered more closely here, because they deviate from this concept; they are adduced only to mark the boundaries of the field which is our real concern.

But what of the genuine translator, who wants to bring those two completely separated persons, his author and his reader, truly together, and who would like to bring the latter to an understanding and enjoyment of the former as correct and complete as possible without inviting him to leave the sphere of his mother tongue — what roads are open to him? In my opinion there are only two. Either the translator leaves the author in peace, as much as possible, and moves the reader towards him; or he leaves the reader in peace, as much as possible, and moves the author towards him. The two roads are so completely separate from each other that one or the other must be followed as closely as possible, and that a highly unreliable result would proceed from any mixture, so that it is to be feared that author and reader would not meet at all. The difference between the two methods, and the fact that they stand in this relationship, must be immediately obvious. For in the first case the translator tries, by means of his work, to replace for the reader the understanding of the original language that the reader does not have. He tries to communicate to the readers the same image, the same impression he himself has gained — through his knowledge of the original language — of the work as it stands, and in doing so he tries to move the readers towards his point of view, which is essentially foreign to them. But if the translation wants to let its Roman author, for instance, speak the way he would have spoken to Germans if he had been German, it does not merely move the author to where the translator stands, because to him he does not speak German, but Latin; rather it drags him directly into the world of the German readers and transforms him into their equal — and that, precisely, is the other case. The first translation will be perfect in its kind when one can say that if the author had learnt German as well as the translator has learnt Latin he would not have translated the work he originally wrote in Latin any differently than the translator has done. But the second, which does not show the author as he himself would have translated but as he, as a German, would have originally written in German, can have no other measure of perfection than if it could be certified that, could all German readers be changed into experts and contemporaries of the author, the original would have meant exactly the same to them as what the translation means to them now — that the author has changed himself into a German. This method is obviously meant by all those who use the formula that one should translate an author in such a way as he himself would have written in German. From this opposition it is immediately obvious how different the procedure must be in every detail, and how, if one tried to switch methods in the course of one and the same project, everything would become unintelligible as well as unpalatable. I merely would like to add that there cannot be a third method, with a precisely delimited goal, over and above these two. The two separated parties must either meet at a certain point in the middle, and that will always be the translator, or one must completely join up with the other, and of these two possibilities only the first belongs to the field of translation; the other would be realized if, in our case, the German readers totally mastered Latin, or rather if that language totally mastered them, to the extent that it actually transformed them. Whatever is said about translation following the letter and translation following the sense, faithful translation and free translation, and whatever other expressions may have gained currency: even though there are supposedly various methods, they must be reducible to the two methods mentioned above — though if we want to talk about virtues and mistakes in this context, the faithful translation which follows the sense or the translation which is too free or too literal will not be the same according to one method as it is according to the other. It is therefore my intention to put aside all problems related to this matter, which have been discussed among specialists, and to observe only the most general features of these two methods, in order to show what the peculiar advantages and disadvantages of each are, as well as the limits of their applicability, and in what respect each best attains the goal of translation. After such a general survey, two things would remain to be done to which this essay is the introduction only. A set of rules could be designed for the two methods, taking into consideration the different genres of speech, and the best attempts which have been made according to either point of view could be compared and judged; this would clarify matters even more. But I must leave both tasks to others, or at least to another occasion.

The method which tries to give the reader the impression he would obtain as a German from reading the original work in the original language must of course first define what kind of understanding of the original language it wants to imitate. For there is one kind it should not imitate and one kind it cannot imitate. The first is a school-like type of understanding which laboriously bungles itself through separate parts, possessed by an attitude close to loathing, and which therefore never gains a clear overview of the whole, a living comprehension of its connections. When the more educated part of a nation has, as a whole, no experience of a more intimate penetration into foreign languages, let those who have progressed beyond this be saved by their good genius from trying to produce this kind of translation. For if they wanted to take their own understanding as a measure, they themselves would be little understood and have little impact, but if their translation were to represent common understanding, their ungainly work could not be shoved off the stage fast enough. In such a time free imitations should first awaken and sharpen the desire for the foreign, and paraphrases prepare a more general understanding, to open the way for future translations. But there is another understanding, which no translator is able to imitate. Let us think of such wonderful people as nature produces every so often, as if to show that it is also capable of destroying the barriers of the common in isolated cases: people who feel such a peculiar kinship with a foreign existence that they completely live and think in a foreign language and its products, and while they are totally occupied with a foreign world they let their own language and their own world become totally foreign. Or let us think of such people who are as it were destined to represent the power of language in its totality, and for whom all languages that they can attain in any way have the same value; in fact, they dress up in them as if they had been born into them. These people have reached a point at which the value of translation becomes nil, for since there is not even the slightest influence of the mother tongue in their perception of foreign works, and since they by no means become conscious of their understanding in their mother tongue but are immediately and totally at home in the original language itself, they also do not feel any incommensurability between their thinking and the language in which they read; it is therefore obvious that no translation can reach or portray their understanding. And just as it would be like pouring water into the sea, or even into wine, if one were to translate for them, just so they are wont to smile with sympathy from their great height — and rightly so — on the attempts made in this field. For if the audience that translations are made for were their equal, then of course we would not have to go to all this trouble. Translation therefore relates to a state of affairs in between these two extremes, and the translator must therefore take as his aim to give his reader the same image and the same delight which the reading of the work in the original language would afford any reader educated in such a way that we call him, in the better sense of the word, the lover and the expert, the type of reader who is familiar with the foreign language while it yet always remains foreign to him: he no longer has to think every single part in his mother tongue, as schoolboys do, before he can grasp the whole, but he is still conscious of the difference between that language and his mother tongue, even where he enjoys the beauty of a foreign work in total peace. Granted, the definition and the operational radius of this type of translation remain unsettled enough, even after we have settled this point. We can only see this: as the desire to translate can originate only when a certain ability for intercourse with foreign languages is widespread among the educated part of the population, just so the art will develop and the aim be set higher and higher, the more love and knowledge of foreign products of the spirit spread and increase among those elements of the population who have exercised and trained their ears, without specializing in the knowledge of languages. But at the same time we cannot hide from ourselves the fact that the more readers are predisposed towards this kind of translation, the higher the difficulties of the enterprise pile up, all the more so if efforts are concentrated on the most characteristic products of a nation's art and scholarship, which are the most important objects for the translator. For, as language is an historical fact, there can be no right sense for it without a sense of history. Languages are not invented, and all arbitrary work in them and on them is stupid; but they are gradually discovered, and scholarship and art are the powers through which this discovery is promoted and brought to fulfilment. Every excellent spirit in whom a part of the ideas of a nation shapes itself in a peculiar way in one of those two forms works in language and influences it to that end, and his works must, therefore, also contain part of that language's history. This places the translator of scholarly work before great, indeed often insurmountable difficulties, for whoever reads an excellent work of that kind in the original language will not easily overlook its influence on language, provided he is equipped with sufficient knowledge. He notices which words, which combinations still appear to him in the first splendour of novelty; he observes how they insinuate themselves into the language through the special needs of the author's spirit and his expressive power; and this type of observation very essentially determines the impression he derives. It is therefore the task of translation to transplant that very same impression into its reader; otherwise he loses part of what was intended for him — often a very important part. But how can this be achieved? To start with particulars: how often will a new word in the original best correspond to one which is old and used in our language, so that the translator would have to replace it with a foreign content, and therefore would have to move into the field of imitation, if he wanted to reveal the language-shaping aspect of the work? How often, when he can render the new by means of the new, will the word which is closest in etymology and derivation not render the sense most faithfully, and will he nonetheless have to awaken other connotations if he does not want to obscure the immediate connection? He will have to console himself with the thought that he can make good his omissions where the author did use old and well-known words, and that he will therefore achieve in general what he is unable to achieve in every particular case. But if one considers the word-shaping work produced by a master in its totality, his use of related words and roots of words in a whole number of interrelated writings: how does the translator propose to find a happy solution here, since the system of concepts and their signs in his language is totally different from that of the original language, and since roots of words do not cover each other in parallel, but rather cut through each other in the most amazing directions? It is therefore impossible for the translator's use of language to be as coherent as that of his author. In this case he will have to be content to achieve in particular what he cannot achieve in general. With his readers he will reach the understanding that they will not think of the other writings as stringently as the readers of the original would, but rather consider each one on its own, and that they should in fact praise him if he manages to salvage similarity with regard to the more important objects in particular writings, or even in parts of them only, so that one single word does not acquire a number of totally different deputies, or that a colourful variety reigns in the translation where the original has strictly related expressions throughout. These difficulties reveal themselves for the most part in the field of scholarship; there are others, and they are by no means smaller in size, in the field of poetry and more artistic prose, in which the musical element of language, which becomes apparent in rhythm and change of tone, also has a specific and higher meaning. Everyone feels that the finest spirit, the highest magic or art in their most perfect products is lost, or even destroyed, when this is not taken into account. Hence, what a sensible reader of the original observes as peculiar in this respect, as intentional, as influencing tone and mood of feeling, as decisive for the mimic and musical accompaniment of speech, that will also have to be translated by our translator. But how often — indeed it is almost a miracle if one does not have to say always — will rhythmical and melodic fidelity not be locked in irreconcilable combat with dialectic and grammatical fidelity! How difficult it is to avoid sacrificing something, now here, now there, in the swinging to and fro, and to avoid what is often exactly the wrong result. How difficult it is even for the translator to restore to his author impartially, when he has occasion for it, what he has had to take away from him before, and not, even unconsciously, to fall into a persistent one-sidedness because his inclination goes out to one artistic element above the others. For if his taste in works of art gravitates more towards ethical subject matter and the way in which it is treated he will be less inclined to see where he has failed to do justice to the metrical and musical elements of the form, and he will, instead of thinking of replacing them, be satisfied with a translation which is more and more diluted in the easy and the semi-paraphrastic. Should the translator on the other hand happen to be a metrician or a musician he will put the logical elements last, in order to grasp the musical element completely, and as he sinks deeper and deeper into this one-sidedness his work will become less and less felicitous, and on comparing his translation in general with the original one will find that he comes closer and closer — without noticing it — to that schoolboyish inadequacy which loses the whole in the parts; a totally different overall impression must be the result if he changes what is light and naturally rendered in one language into heavy and objectionable expressions in the other, merely for love of the material similarity of rhythm and tone.

Still other difficulties appear when the translator reflects on his relationship with the language he is writing in and on the relationship of his translation with his other works. If we except those miraculous masters to whom many languages are as one, or to whom a learned language is even more natural than their mother tongue — those for whom one cannot translate, as has been said before — all others retain a sense of the strange, no matter how fluently they read a foreign language. How should the translator transfer this feeling — that they have something foreign before them — to the readers whom he offers a translation in their mother tongue? Of course you will say that the answer to this riddle has been given long ago, and that the problem has often been solved more than well enough in our case, for the more closely the translation follows the turns taken by the original, the more foreign it will seem to the reader. That may well be true, and it is easy enough to ridicule this position in general. But if this joy is not to be purchased too cheaply, if the most magisterial is not to be thrown out in one bath with the worst and the most schoolboyish, it will have to be admitted that an indispensable requirement of this method of translation is a feeling for language which is not only not colloquial, but also causes us to suspect that it has not grown in total freedom but rather has been bent towards a foreign likeness; and it must be admitted that to do this artfully and with measure, without disadvantage to one's language or oneself, is probably the greatest difficulty our translator has to overcome. The attempt seems to be the strangest form of humiliation a writer who is not a bad writer could impose upon himself. Who would not like to permit his mother tongue to stand forth everywhere in the most universally appealing beauty each genre is capable of? Who would not rather sire children who are their parents' pure effigy, and not bastards? Who would willingly force himself to appear in movements less light and elegant than those he is capable of, to seem brutal and stiff, at least at times, and to shock the reader as much as is necessary to keep him aware of what he is doing? Who would put up with being considered clumsy, by trying to keep as close to the foreign language as his own language allows? Who would suffer being accused, like those parents who abandon their children to acrobats, of bending his mother tongue to foreign and unnatural dislocations instead of skilfully exercising it in its own natural gymnastics? Finally, who would like to be smiled upon with compassion by the greatest experts and masters who could not understand his laborious and ill-considered German if they did not supplement it with their Greek and Latin. These are the sacrifices every translator must needs take upon himself, these are the dangers he exposes himself to when he does not observe the finest line in his attempts to keep the tone of the language foreign — and he never escapes from them altogether because everyone draws that line a little differently. If he also thinks of the inevitable influence of habit in addition to this, he may fear that much that is raw, that does not really belong, will insinuate itself into his free and original production via translation, and that habit will somewhat blunt in him the tender sense of the natural feeling for language. And should he think of the great host of imitators and of the slowness and mediocrity that reign among his writing audience, he will be horrified at the amount of unlawfulness, of genuine stiffness and clumsiness, of linguistic corruption of all kinds perpetrated by others, and yet he will probably have to answer for it, for no doubt only the best and the worst will not attempt to derive a false advantage from his endeavours. This type of complaint — that such a translation must of necessity be harmful to the purity of language and its peaceful development — has often been heard. Even if we want to put it to one side with the consolation that there will be advantages, too, to counterbalance these disadvantages, and that, since all good is mixed with evil, true wisdom is to acquire as much as possible of the former and to take over the least possible of the latter, some consequences must, in any case, be drawn from this difficult task of representing what is foreign in one's mother tongue. First, this method of translating cannot thrive equally well in all languages, but only in those which are not the captives of too strict a bond of classical expression outside of which all is reprehensible. Such bonded languages should expect a broadening of their sphere by having themselves spoken by foreigners who need more than their mother tongue; they will be perfectly suited to this. They may incorporate foreign works by means of imitations, or even translations of the other type; they must, however, relinquish this type to languages which are freer, in which innovations and deviations are tolerated to a greater extent, in such a way that their accumulation may, under certain circumstances, generate a certain characteristic mode of expression. Another obvious consequence is that this type of translation has no value whatsoever if it is practised only by chance and in isolated instances in a given language. For that obviously falls short of the aim that a foreign spirit should blow towards the reader; on the contrary, if he is to be given a notion, albeit a very weak one, of the original language and of what the work owes to it, so that his failure to understand that language is somewhat made up for, he must not only be given the totally vague impression that what he reads does not sound completely familiar; he must also be made to feel that it sounds like something different, yet definite. But that will only be possible if he is able to make massive comparisons. If he has read something he knows has been translated from other modern languages and something else which has been translated from classical languages, and if they have been translated in the sense described above, he will acquire an ear with which to distinguish between the old and the newer. But he will have to have read much more if he is to be able to distinguish between works of Greek and Roman origin, or Italian and Spanish. And yet even this is hardly the highest goal; on the contrary, the reader of the translation will become the equal of the better reader of the original only when he is able first to acquire an impression of the particular spirit of the author as well as that of the language in the work and by and by to develop a definite grasp of it. He can do so only through his powers of observation, but a much greater volume of comparisons is indispensable if he is to be able to exercise those powers. These comparisons are not available if only isolated works of masters of isolated genres are sporadically translated into a language. In this way even the most educated readers can achieve only a very deficient knowledge of what is foreign by means of translation, and it is inconceivable that they would be able to reach any judgment of either the translation or the original. This method of translation must therefore be applied extensively, a transplantation of whole literatures into a language, and it makes sense and is of value only to a nation that has the definite inclination to appropriate what is foreign. Isolated works of this type are of value only as precursors of a more generally evolving and developing willingness to adopt this procedure. If they fail to arouse this, things will work against them in the language and the spirit of the time; they can then only appear as mistaken attempts and have little or no success in themselves. But even if this way should prevail, it should not complacently be expected that a work of this nature, be it ever so excellent, will gather general approval. Since many factors have to be considered and many difficulties resolved, it is inevitable that different opinions should develop as to which parts of the task should be considered of primary and which of secondary importance. Thus different schools, so to speak, will arise among the masters, and different parties among the audience as followers of those schools, and even though the method is basically the same, different translations of the same work, undertaken from different points of view, will be able to exist side by side and we shall not really be able to say that one is, as a whole, more or less perfect than another; certain parts only will be more successful in one version, and others in another, and not until they are all taken together and related to each other and it becomes clear how one translator attaches particular value to this approximation to the original and another to that, or how one translator exercises particular forbearance towards what is native, not until then will they completely exhaust their task, for each one in itself will always be of relative and subjective value only.

These are the difficulties which beset this method and the imperfections essentially inherent in it. But once we have conceded them, we must acknowledge the attempt itself and cannot deny its merit. It rests on two conditions: that understanding foreign works should be a thing known and desired and that the native language should be allowed a certain flexibility. Where these conditions are fulfilled this type of translation becomes a natural phenomenon, influencing the whole evolution of a culture and giving a certain pleasure as it is given a certain value.

But what of the opposite method, which does not expect any labour or exertion on the part of the reader, aspiring to bring the foreign author into his immediate proximity as if by magic, and to show the work as it would have been if the author himself had originally written it in the reader's language. This requirement has not seldom been formulated as the one a true translator would have to fulfil and as being of a much higher and more perfect nature when compared to the other; isolated attempts have been made, even masterpieces perhaps, which have clearly taken this for their goal. Let us now find out what they are like, and whether it would perhaps not be a good thing if this procedure, which has without a doubt been more rarely applied up to now, were to be followed more frequently and to supplant the other, which is of a dubious nature and unsatisfactory in many ways.

It is immediately obvious that the translator's language has nothing at all to fear from this method. The first rule he must follow is not to allow himself anything – considering the relationship in which his work stands to a foreign language – which would not also be allowed in an original work of the same genre in his native tongue. Indeed, it is his duty above all to observe at least the same care for the purity and perfection of language, to strive after the same light and natural style for which his author is famous in the original language. It is equally true that, if we want to make clear to our compatriots what an author meant for his language, we cannot think of a better formula than to introduce him speaking in such a way as we imagine he would have spoken in ours, especially when the level of development at which he found his language is similar to the level our language happens to have reached. We can imagine, in a certain sense, how Tacitus would have spoken if he had been a German, or more accurately how a German would speak who meant the same to our language as Tacitus to his — and good luck to him who is able to imagine this so vividly that he can actually make him speak. But whether this would happen if he let him say the same things Roman Tacitus said in the Latin language is another question which cannot easily be answered in the affirmative. For it is one thing to grasp correctly the influence a man has exerted on his native language and somehow to show it, and quite another to want to know how his thoughts and their expression would have shaped themselves if he had originally been wont to think and express himself in another language. Can anyone who is convinced of the internal and essential identity of thought and expression — and the whole art of all understanding of speech and therefore also of all translation is based on this conviction — can such a person want to sever a man from the language he was born into, and think that a man, or even just his train of thought, could be one and the same in two languages? Or if they are, in a certain way, different, can he presume to dissolve speech down to its very core, separate from that the part played by language, and let this core, as if through a new and almost chemical process, combine with the essence and the power of another language? To do this one would obviously have to separate neatly everything which is, in a man's written work, influenced by whatever he may have spoken and heard in his mother tongue from childhood on, after which one would have to add, so to speak, to that same man's naked, peculiar way of thought — perceived as directed towards a certain object — whatever would have been the influence of whatever he might have spoken and heard in the foreign language from the beginning of his life onwards, or from his first acquaintance with it, until he had become capable of original thinking and expression in it. This will be possible only when it becomes possible to combine organic products successfully by means of a chemical process. Indeed it might be said that the aim of translating in such a way as the author would have originally written in the language of the translation is not only out of reach, but also null and void in itself, for whoever acknowledges the shaping power of language, as it is one with the peculiar character of a nation, must concede that every most excellent human being has acquired his knowledge, as well as the possibility of expressing it, in and through language and that no one therefore adheres to his language mechanically, as if he were strapped into it, to use a superficial simile, and that no one could change languages in his thinking as he pleases, the way one can easily change a span of horses and replace it with another; rather everyone produces original work in his mother tongue only, so that the question cannot even be raised of how he would have written his works in another language. Everyone will of course adduce two cases against this, and they occur often enough.

First, there obviously is such a thing as the ability to write in languages other than one's native tongue, indeed even to philosophize in them and to write poetry in them — not just in isolated exceptions, even though these occur as well, but also in general. Why then should one not, to acquire a more reliable yardstick, confer this ability, in thought, on every author one wants to translate?

Because this ability is of such a nature that it is present only in those situations in which the same thing could not have been said at all in the native language, or at least not by the same person. If we go back in time to the point where the Romance languages began to develop, who can say which language was native to people at that moment? And who will want to deny that Latin was more of a mother tongue than the vernaculars for those who were drawn to scholarly aspirations? This goes much deeper for isolated needs and activities of the mind. As long as the mother tongue has not been developed for them, that language from which those directions of the spirit have communicated themselves to an evolving nation remains the partial mother tongue. Grotius and Leibniz could not write philosophy in Dutch or in German, at least not without becoming totally different people. Indeed, even when that root is completely dried out and the scion has been completely torn off the old trunk, whoever is not at the same time a being who shapes and uproots language will needs be often adhere to a foreign tongue, either by choice or because he is forced to do so by subordinate causes. Our great king [Frederick II of Prussia] received all his finer and higher thoughts in a foreign language, which he had most intimately appropriated for this field. He was incapable of producing in German the literature and philosophy he produced in French. It is to be deplored that the great preference for England which dominated a part of the family could not have taken the direction of familiarizing him from childhood on with the English language, whose last golden age was then in bloom, and which is so much closer to German. But we may hope that he would have preferred to produce literature and philosophy in Latin, rather than in French, if he had enjoyed a strict scholarly education. In so far as this is subject to particular conditions, in so far as people do not produce in just any foreign language but only in a definite one, and then only what they were not able to produce in their mother tongue, it does not prove anything in favour of a method of translation which wishes to show how someone would have written in another language what he has, in effect, written in his mother tongue.

But the second case, that of original reading and writing in a foreign language, seems to be more favourable to this method. For who will deny our courtiers and diplomats that they have immediately thought in the same language whatever sweet nothings they let pass their lips in foreign tongues, without first translating them from poor old German in their mind? And as it is their claim to fame to be able to say these sweet nothings and dainty phrases with the same excellence in many tongues, they must of course think in all these languages with the same ease, and everyone will know how the other would have said in Italian what he has just said in French. But these speeches do not belong in the realm in which thoughts grow forcefully from the deep root of a particular language; they are more like the pepperwort that a man of artifice manages to grow on a white cloth, not in any soil. These speeches are neither the sacred seriousness of language nor its beautiful well-measured game; rather, as nations appear to mix in our time to a greater extent than they did before, the market-place is everywhere and these are conversations of the market-place, whether they are social or literary or political, and really do not belong in the translator's domain but rather in that of the interpreter. If these conversations are flicked together to a greater whole and put on paper, as sometimes happens, then that type of work which takes place totally in the light and lovely life, without opening up any depth of being or preserving any particular traits of a nation, can be translated according to those rules — but that type of work only, because only that type could just as well have been written in another language. And this rule should not apply beyond, except possibly to the prefaces or introductions of deeper and more noble works which often belong entirely to the domain of light social life. But the more the special features of a nation and, perhaps even beyond that, the shape of a time long past adhere to the simple thoughts contained in a work and to the relationships between them, the more that rule simply loses its mening. For as true as it is in many ways that a man is in a certain sense educated and a citizen of the world only through his knowledge of various languages, we must concede that just as we do not consider that type of world citizenship real which supplants love for one's country at critical moments, just so such a general love which desires to equate any language old or new with the national language for both colloquial and higher usage is not a true and really civilizing love in the field of languages. Just as a man must decide to belong to one country, just so he must adhere to one language, or he will float without any bearings above an unpleasant middle ground. It is right that even now Latin is being written among us as the language of officialdom, to keep alive the consciousness that this has been the scholarly and sacred mother tongue of our ancestors; it is good that this should also happen in the field of the common European economy, to make commerce easier; but in that case, too, it will succeed only to the extent that the object is everything for such a representation and that one's own opinion and the way in which one combines objects count for very little. The same holds true for French. Whoever is forced to write such a language for official purposes will be very conscious of the fact that his thoughts are German in their initial origin and that he merely begins to translate them very early on, while the embryo is still shaping itself; and whoever subjects himself to this for the sake of scholarship will find himself translating at ease, in an open and natural way, only where he feels himself totally in the power of the object. There is, of course, in addition to this also the writing of Latin or French as a free pastime, and if the object of this exercise were really to produce as well in a foreign language as in one's own and with the same originality, I would not hesitate to declare it to be an evil and magic art, like that of being someone's double, by means of which men not only attempted to ridicule the laws of nature, but also to confuse others. But this is not the case; rather this pastime is merely a refined mimic game with which to while away the hours pleasantly in the outer courts of scholarship and art. Production in a foreign language is not original; rather remembrance of a certain writer or even of the style of a certain period, which represents a general person, appear before the soul, so to speak, almost as a living outside image, and the imitation thereof guides production and defines it. This is also the reason why so rarely anything of real value comes into being in this way, except for mimic accuracy, and one can enjoy one's favourite piece all the more harmlessly because the person mimicked can be seen clearly enough everywhere. But if, contrary to nature and morality, someone has formally become a deserter to his mother tongue and given himself to another, it is not artificial and imputed scorn when he asserts that he cannot move in it any more; it is merely a justification he owes himself that his nature is really a marvel of nature contrary to all rules and order, and a reassurance to others that at least he does not have a double emanation as ghosts do.

But we have dealt with what is strange at too great length, and it must have seemed as if we have been talking about writing in foreign languages instead of translating from them. The case is this. If it is not possible to write something in a foreign language worthy of — and in need of — translation as art, or if this is at least a rare and miraculous exception, we cannot set up as a rule for translation that it should imagine how the writer himself would have written precisely what he has written in the language of the translator, for there is no fulness of examples of bilingual authors from which an analogy could be drawn for the translator to follow; rather he will be left almost totally to his own imagination for all works which do not resemble light entertainment or commercial transactions. Indeed, what can be the objection if a translator were to tell a reader: Here is the book just as the author would have written it if he had written in German, and if the reader were to reply: I am much obliged to you, in the same way as if you had brought me the picture of the author just as he would have looked if his mother had conceived him with another father? For if the writer's particular spirit is the mother of works belonging to scholarship and art in a higher sense, his national language is the father. Artificialities, on the other hand, lay claim to secret insights that nobody has, and only as a game can one enjoy them without inhibition.

That the applicability of this method is severely limited, indeed that it is almost equal to zero in the field of translation, is borne out best when one views the insuperable difficulties that entangle it as far as isolated branches of scholarship and art are concerned. We must admit that there are in colloquial usage only a few words in a language which correspond completely to words in another, so that one might be used in all the cases in which the other is used and that one would produce exactly the same effect as the other in the same constellation; how much more true is this for all concepts, the more a philosophical essence is added to them, and hence it is most true of genuine philosophy. Here more than anywhere else every language, in spite of differing contemporary and successive opinions, contains within it a system of concepts which, precisely because they touch each other in the same language, because they connect and complement each other, are a Whole whose isolated parts do not correspond to any in the system of other languages, not even if we except

God and Is, the original noun and the original verb. For even what is commonly held to be general is illuminated and coloured by language, even though it lies outside the boundaries of the particular. The wisdom of every individual must be dissolved in this system of language. Everyone partakes of what is there, and everyone helps to bring to light what is not yet there but prefigured. In this way only is the wisdom of the individual alive and can it really rule his existence which he completely summarizes in that language. If, therefore, the translator of a philosophical writer does not want to make the decision to bend the language of the translation as far as possible towards that of the original in order to communicate as far as possible an impression of the system of concepts developed in it, if he had rather make his author speak as if he had originally fashioned thoughts and speech in another language, what choice does he have, in view of the dissimilarity of elements in both languages: he must either paraphrase — in which case he fails to achieve his aim, for a paraphrase can never look like what has originally been produced in the same language — or he must transpose his author's entire knowledge and wisdom into the conceptual system of another language, and therefore change all isolated parts, in which case it is hard to see how the wildest arbitrariness might be kept within bounds. Indeed, it should be said that no one who has even the slightest respect for philosophical endeavours can allow himself to be drawn into so loose a game. I leave it to Plato to justify my going on from the philosopher to the writer of comedies. This genre is, from the linguistic point of view, closest to the domain of colloquial conversation. The whole representation is alive in the morals of the people and the time, and those in turn mirror themselves perfectly, in the most lively way, in language. Lightness and naturalness in elegance are its prime virtue, and that is precisely the reason why the difficulties of translating according to the method we have just considered are immense. For any approximation to a foreign language is bound to harm those virtues of diction. If the translation wants to make a playwright speak as if he had originally written in its language, it will not be able to let him show many things because they are not native to its people and therefore also have no symbol in their language. In this case the translator must consequently either cut them out completely, and in so doing destroy the power and form of the whole, or else he must replace them. It is obvious that if the formula is faithfully followed in this field, it will either lead to pure imitation or to an even more clearly repulsive and confusing mixture of translation and imitation which cruelly bounces the reader back and forth like a ball between the foreign world and his own, between the author's wit and imagination and that of the translator; he will not derive any pure pleasure from this, but in the end he will certainly be left with enough dizziness and frustration. On the other hand the translator who follows the other method is not required to undertake such self-willed changes, because his reader must always remember that the author lived in a different world and wrote in a different language. He is bound only by the admittedly difficult art of supplying knowledge of this strange world in the shortest and most efficient way and letting the greater lightness and naturalness of the original shine through everywhere. These two examples taken from opposite extremes of art and scholarship show clearly how little the real aim of all translation, the unadulterated enjoyment, within the limits of the possible, of foreign works, can be achieved by means of a method which insists on breathing the spirit of a language which is alien to it into the translated work. Add to this that every language also has its own peculiarities of rhythm, for prose as well as for poetry, and that, once the fiction is to be established that the author could also have written in the translator's language, one would also have to let him appear in the rhythm of that language, which would disfigure his work even more and limit even further the knowledge of its particular character which translation provides.

This fiction, on which alone rests the theory of translation now under discussion, goes far beyond the aim of that activity. As seen from the first point of view, translation is a matter of necessity for a nation in which only a small minority of people are able to acquire sufficient knowledge of foreign languages, whereas a greater minority has a desire to enjoy foreign works. Should the latter be totally subsumed under the former, all translation would be useless, and it would be difficult to have anyone take on that thankless labour. Not so from the second point of view. Translation has nothing to do with necessity; rather it is the labour of recklessness and lasciviousness. Let knowledge of foreign languages be as widespread as possible and let access to their noblest works be open to anyone who is competent; it would still be a miraculous endeavour, which would gather around itself more and more increasingly intrigued listeners, if someone were to promise to show us a work of Cicero's or Plato's in the way these authors would have written it directly in German at the present moment. And if someone were to bring us to the point that we would do this not only in our mother tongue but also in another, foreign language, he would obviously be a master of the difficult and almost impossible art of dissolving the spirits of languages into each other. One can see, however, that this would not be translation, strictly speaking, and that its goal would not be the most precise possible enjoyment of the works themselves; it would become more and more of an imitation and only he could truly enjoy such a work or piece of art who was already immediately and independently familiar with those authors. And the true aim could only be, in particular, to show a similar relationship in different languages between many expressions and combinations and certain inner features, and in general to illuminate language with the particular spirit of a foreign master, but one who is completely separated and cut off from his own language. As the former is only an artificial and elegant game, and as the latter rests on a fiction which it is almost impossible to put into practice, it is understandable why this type of translation is only sparingly applied in a few attempts which serve to demonstrate that it cannot be applied more widely. It is also understandable why only excellent masters who may presume the miraculous could work according to this method; only those who have already done their duty by the world and may therefore allow themselves to be drawn into an exciting and somewhat dangerous game are entitled to do so. One understands all the more easily why the masters who feel capable of trying such a thing look down with a certain compassion on the busyness of those other translators. For they believe that they alone are engaged in that beautiful and fine art, and any others seem to be much closer to the interpreter in so far as they, too, serve a need, albeit a slightly nobler one. Such interpreters seem to be all the more deserving of pity since they invest much more labour and art than could possibly be justified in a subordinate and thankless business. Hence the masters are always ready to advise that one should get by with paraphrases as much as possible, the way interpreters do in difficult or dubious cases, and that one should not produce this type of translation.

Well then? Should we share this opinion and follow this advice? The ancients obviously translated little in that most real sense and most moderns, deterred by the difficulties of true translation, also seem to be satisfied with imitation and paraphrase. Who would want to contend that nothing has ever been translated into French from the classical languages or from the Germanic languages! But even though we Germans are perfectly willing to listen to this advice, we should not follow it. An inner necessity, in which a peculiar calling of our people expresses itself clearly enough, has driven us to translating *en masse*; we cannot go back and we must go on. Just as our soil itself has no doubt become richer and more fertile and our climate milder and more pleasant only after much transplantation of foreign flora, just so we sense that our language, because we exercise it less owing to our Nordic sluggishness, can thrive in all its freshness and completely develop its own power only through the most many-sided contacts with what is foreign. And coincidentally our nation may be destined, because of its respect for what is foreign and its nature which is one of mediation, to carry all the treasures of foreign arts and scholarship, together with its own, in its language, to unite them into a great historical whole, so to speak, which would be preserved in the centre and heart of Europe, so that, with the help of our language, whatever beauty the most different times have brought forth can be enjoyed by all people, as purely and perfectly as is possible for a foreigner. This appears indeed to be the real historical aim of translation in general, as we are used to it now. To this end, however, only the method we have discussed first should be followed. Art must learn, as much as possible, to overcome its difficulties, which we have not tried to hide. We have made a good beginning, but the greater part of the work still remains to be done. Many exercises and attempts must be gone through first, in this field as in any other, before a few excellent works come into being, and much shines at the outset that is later supplanted by what is better. The extent to which individual artists have already in part overcome these difficulties and in part skirted them in a felicitous way is evidenced in many examples. And even if there are those working in the field who are less able, we should not fear great harm to our language from their endeavours. For it must be established at the outset that there is, in a language in which translation is practised to such an extent, a field proper to translators, and that much should be allowed to them which should not be permitted to show itself elsewhere. Whoever further transplants these innovations without authorization will find a few imitators only, or none, and if we want to close the account after not too short a period of time we can rely on the assimilating process of language to discard again whatever has been accepted only because of a passing need and does not really correspond to its nature. On the other hand we should not fail to acknowledge that much of what is powerful and beautiful in our language has in part developed through translations or has in part been drawn from obscurity by them. We speak too little and make, proportionately, too much conversation, and it cannot be denied that for quite a while our style had evolved too far in that direction and that translation has contributed more than a little to the re-establishment of a stricter style. If ever the time should come in which we have a public life out of which develops a sociability of greater merit and truer to language, and in which free space is gained for the talent of the orator, we shall be less in need of translation for the development of language. If only that time might come before we have rounded with dignity the whole circle of difficulties in translation.

[Friedrich Schleiermacher, "Ueber die verschiedenen Methoden des Uebersezens" (1813), as printed in FS, *Sämmtliche Werke*, Dritte Abtheilung (*Zur Philosophie*), Bd. II (Berlin: Reimer, 1838), 207-245. Reprinted in Störig, 38-70.]

Part Two: Internal Criticism of the Tradition

Internal Criticism of the Tradition: Introductory Remarks

Internal criticism of the tradition, foreshadowed by Friedrich Schlegel's attack on Voss's sacrosanct translation, starts in earnest with Jakob Grimm. Most of it is justified; what is not provides, at the very least, perspective and counterpoint. Yet it tends to obscure the main insight gained by the tradition before it became stagnant as a result of growing insistence on the atomization of the original and an aggressive, imperialist mutation of the nationalism which has always been one of its components. This mutation finds its most radical expression in Friedrich Nietzsche, who, ironically, appears to vindicate the French rather than the German example, and Karl Vossler, who does not shrink from using plainly militaristic language.

The tradition holds that translation ". . . is the most intensive form of reading, namely of a reading which becomes itself creative and productive again, via understanding, explanation, and criticism. Since early Romantic opinion holds, however, that original art itself is merely reproductive, there is no qualitative distinction left between reproductive translation and reproductive original writing. The less so since, to the early Romantics, literature was not something objectively finished, but rather something which ought to be progressively widened and perfected . . ." (Huyssen, 145). In short, "Translation appears, beyond criticism, as the next higher and final step of philological hermeneutics" (Huyssen, 143).

Schleiermacher's translationese represents an attempt to create a separate sub-language for use in translated literature only. This language would be, at one and the same time, cut off from the living language and yet somehow connected with it. The attempt to sever the theory of literary translation from the theory of literature itself has, unfortunately, been far more successful. Literary translation has been relegated to the dubious limbo of "craftsmanship" and "specialization", which can claim only the most tenuous connections with literary scholarship. Both literary scholarship and the theory of literary translation have had to pay a high price for this state of affairs. "I would like to voice the suspicion that the stagnation of German translation theory after the Romantic era should essentially be blamed on the fact that the connections between translation and criticism, which the brothers Schlegel had focused on for the first time, were lost sight of . . ." (Huyssen, 111).

Schopenhauer's elitist insistence on the grammatical perfection of classical

languages and on the theoretical impossibility of translation started the movement towards extreme literalism in actual practice. For Schopenhauer the
philosopher, classical languages, which he rather inexplicably equates with
Latin, rather than Greek, for instance, or Sanskrit, are primarily a means of
developing one's own mind and, consequently, one's own personal powers of
expression. Translation is no longer designed to improve *langue*, but rather to
perfect *parole*. Schopenhauer's insistence on polyglottism overlooks the fact
that man's life span is too short to absorb even all of the most "perfect"
languages. Since languages were, to him, as to Leibniz, primarily repositories of
concepts, it followed that comparisons between different languages would
inevitably lead to what would amount to a freeing of pure concepts from the
languages in which they are held captive.

Walter Benjamin applied this idea, transmuted by cabalistic mysticism, to all
languages, in the hope of restoring a "pure" language in the process. His
theory, which is also indebted to Schleiermacher and the more obscure side of
German hermeneuticism, lapses into mystical vagaries, whereas his practice is
remarkably conservative.

Ulrich von Wilamowitz-Moellendorff reverses the elitist attitude taken by
Schopenhauer. Precisely because the classical ideal is so valuable to him, it
should be shared with everyone by means of translation. Wilamowitz under-
mines the prejudices against translation inspired by Schopenhauer and rein-
states the principle of equivalence of effect. He criticizes both Goethe and A.W.
Schlegel and re-emphasizes the importance of the tradition of the target literature as first pointed out by Friedrich Schlegel. Following Humboldt, he
vindicates the essentially cumulative nature of the task of translating literature.
Wilamowitz also reaffirms the importance of philology for literary translation,
yet at the same time he insists, over and against the dominant idea of literalism,
that philology on its own is not enough. It needs to be supplemented by
inspiration and genuine artistic craftsmanship.

Rudolf Borchardt's demand that translation should restore something to the
original and its language echoes an insight first formulated by Herder. His
attack on the German theorists and practitioners of literary translation during
the era of "pink roses" is reproduced here because one often finds their names
listed in English bibliographies on the subject, rather than those of their much
more profound and influential predecessors, presumably because the timing of
their work coincided with the reawakening of interest in the translation of
literature which characterized the last two decades of Victorian England.

Franz Rosenzweig, finally, vindicates practice over theory by insisting on the
validity of compromise. He reaffirms the insight voiced by Herder, Schleiermacher, and A. W. Schlegel that all speech is translation and stresses that
literary translation is absolutely essential as an antidote against the aggressive,
imperialist nationalism referred to above.

Jakob Grimm, 1785-1863

One might be inclined to believe that our language is especially suitable for translations because of the beautiful tendency towards unadorned simplicity which is so characteristic of it; and so it is, to a certain extent. It would, however, be an exaggeration of the value of the insatiable translations, all too widespread among us, of almost every foreign work of renown, to go so far as to claim that some of them are so successful that they could be used to reconstruct the source text, if it were ever to be lost. I at least must admit that I have no idea as to how from the works of Schlegel or Voss a Shakespeare or a Homer could arise as majestic as the English or the Greek one in their marvellous beauty. What translation entails may be made clear simply by using the same word again; I only have to shift the stress: to trans*late* is to *trans*late, *traducere navem.* Whoever has a talent for navigation, whoever is able to man a ship and lead it with full sail to the opposite shore, still has to land where the air and the soil are different. We translate faithfully, because we allow ourselves to incorporate all the specific traits of the foreign language through osmosis and because we decide to imitate it, but we translate too faithfully, because the forms and the substances of words in two languages can never totally cover each other and one loses what the other gains. Whereas free translations, therefore, only aspire to attain the thought and give up the beauty of the dress, strict translations pedantically strain themselves to weave a copy of the dress, and fall short of the source text whose form and content naturally and spontaneously agree. Imitation of Latin or Greek poetry forces us to squeeze German words together, which leads to the danger of doing violence to the sense. Translated prose tends to become more verbose, which is obvious if you compare it to the source text.

[From Jakob Grimm, "Über das Pedantische in der deutschen Sprache" (1847), as printed in JG, *Kleinere Schriften*, I (Berlin: Dümmler's Verlagshaus, 2. Aufl., 1879). Reprinted in Störig, 108-135.]

Friedrich Nietzsche, 1844-1900

TRANSLATION AS CONQUEST

One can estimate the degree of historical sense that an epoch possesses by observing how it makes translations and tries to appropriate times and books past. The French of Corneille's time, and even those of the time of the Revolution, took hold of Roman antiquity in a way we would no longer dare, because of our more highly developed historical sense. And Roman antiquity itself: with what power and naïveté did it not lay its hand on all that was good and noble in the Greeks. How did they not translate into the contemporary Roman world! How artfully and carelessly did they not rub the dust off the wings of the butterfly of the moment. Horace, for instance, translated Alcaeus or Archilochus in bits and pieces and Propertius translated Callimachus or Philetas (poets of the same rank as Theocritus, if we are *allowed* to judge): what did they care that the real creator had experienced this or that and that he had written traces of it into his poem — as poets they were averse to the antiquarian browser who is the harbinger of historical sense; as poets they did not allow any validity for those very personal things and names and whatever belonged to a town, a coast, an age as its mask and costume, but they quickly replaced them with what was contemporary and Roman. They seem to be asking us "should we not be allowed to breathe our soul into this dead body? for it is dead and how ugly are all things dead!"— they did not know the pleasures of the sense of history; what was past and foreign gave them grief and incited them, as Romans, to Roman conquest. Indeed one conquered, in those days, when translating — not only because history was left out; no, allusions to the present were added and, above all, the name of the original poet was rubbed out and replaced by one's own — there was no sense of thieving in this, but rather the best concience of the *imperium Romanum*.

[From Friedrich Nietzsche, *Die fröhliche Wissenschaft,* as printed in FN, *Werke in drei Bänden* (ed. Karl Schlechta; Darmstadt: Wissenschaftliche Buchgesellschaft, 3. Aufl., 1962). Reprinted in Störig. 136-137.]

Karl Vossler, 1872-1949

TRANSLATION AS CULTURAL IMPERIALISM

Since translating and interpreting have been invented there is no need for any language's taste to give itself up in order to gain advantages from foreign languages. The real meaning and justification of translation in the philosophy of language lie in the preservation of the autonomy of linguistic taste. All translations are made at the instigation of a linguistic community's instinct for self-preservation.

But the masters of translation: enraptured and possessed by this spirit of language they put their will at its service and go out to loot forms, raid the neighbouring languages and literatures as well as those artistic treasures farthest removed in space and time, and with the wolf's hunger of esthetic imperialism they grasp whatever they lust after. In order to keep it, though, to carry it off and integrate it into the linguistic spirit of their nation, they have to break up the foreign form and still save the best and the most profound of it and bring it home unharmed.

Translation is the defensive element in our language. One should regard the artistically perfect translations in a national literature as strategic bulwarks, and value them accordingly. There are the means by which the linguistic genius of a nation defends itself against what is foreign by cunningly stealing from it as much as possible.

[From Karl Vossler, *Geist und Kultur der Sprache* (Heidelberg: Winter, 1925), ch. "Die sprachlichen Gemeinschaften", as reprinted in Störig, 170-193. The book is available in English as *The Spirit of Language in Civilization* (tr. Oscar Loeser: London: Routledge, 1932).]

Arthur Schopenhauer, 1788-1860

EQUIVALENCE AND THE ATOMIZATION OF THE ORIGINAL

One does not find the exact equivalent of every word of one language in another. Hence not all concepts denoted by words of one language are exactly the same as those expressed by another, even though this is often the case, and sometimes with remarkable precision. For the most part they are merely similar and related concepts, different because somehow modified.

Sometimes one language lacks a word for a concept, even though it can be found in most, perhaps all others ... For certain concepts, on the other hand, a word is found in one language, from wich it passes into others ... Sometimes a foreign language expresses a concept with a nuance that our own language does not provide at this time. In this case everyone who is concerned with the precise expression of his thoughts will use the foreign word and ignore the barking of pedantic purists. In all cases in which a slightly different concept is denoted with the same word in one language and in another, the dictionary renders it by means of various related expressions. They all hit its meaning; not concentrically, however, but in various directions, so as to mark the boundaries within which the concept is situated.

On this rests the necessary imperfection of all translations. One can almost never translate a characteristic, poignant, meaningful sentence from one language into another in such a way that it would produce exactly and entirely the same effect. One cannot *translate poems*, only *transpose* them, which is always awkward. Even in mere prose the best translation will relate to the original at the most as a transposition of a certain musical piece into another key. Those who know music know what that means. Therefore all translations remain dead and their style forced, stiff, unnatural — or else they become free, that is, declare themselves satisfied with an *à peu près,* which means they are inaccurate. A library of translations looks like a picture gallery of copies. Translations of the authors of antiquity are the most obvious surrogates, the way coffee made from chicory is a surrogate for real coffee.

It follows that the difficulty in learning a language is mainly that of getting to know every concept for which it has a word, even if one's own language has no word which precisely corresponds to it — as is often the case. It follows that one must map out a number of completely new spheres of concepts in one's mind.

Thus spheres of concepts arise where there were none before. One therefore does not learn words only; one acquires concepts. This is especialy true when one learns classical languages, because the way in which the ancients expressed themselves differs much more from ours than that in which various modern languages express themselves. This is shown in the fact that one has to make use of ways of expression totally different from those the original possesses when one has to translate into Latin. Indeed, one most often has to melt down and recast the thought one has to render in Latin; in this process it is taken apart down to its basic components and then put together again. It is precisely on this that the great challenge posed to the mind by the learning of foreign languages rests. Only after one has rightly grasped all the concepts that the language to be learnt denotes by means of single words, and only if one immediately connects in thought every word in the foreign language with the corresponding concept — if one does not, therefore, first translate the word into one's mother tongue and then think the concept denoted by it, which does not always precisely correspond to the foreign concept, and the same holds true for whole sentences — only then has one grasped *the spirit* of the language one has to learn, and in doing so one has taken an important step towards understanding the nation which speaks it: for as style is related to the spirit of the individual, so language is related to the spirit of the nation. You have mastered a language completely only if you are able to transpose not books, but yourself, into it, so that you are able to communicate in it directly, without losing your individuality, and in such a way that you can be as pleasing to foreigners as to your own countrymen.

People of limited intellectual ability will not easily come to a real mastery of a foreign language: they learn its words, to be sure, but they always use them only in the sense of their approximate equivalent in their mother tongue, and they always keep the phrases and turns of speech peculiar to that mother tongue. They are simply incapable of acquiring the spirit of the foreign language: the real reason for this is that their thinking is not generated by its own means, but that it is, for the most part, borrowed from their mother tongue, whose current phrases and turns of speech take the place of their own thoughts; hence they always use only outworn turns of speech in their own language and put them together so awkwardly that one realizes how imperfectly they understand their meaning and how little their whole thinking goes beyond words, so that it is not much more than parroting. For opposite reasons the originality of turns of speech and the individual accuracy of each expression used to each situation is an infallible mark of the superior mind.

It will be clear from all this that new concepts which will give a meaning to new signs originate when one learns a new language; that concepts which together made up only a further and therefore vaguer concept because there was only *one* word available for them are differentiated; that relationships unknown before are discovered because the foreign language denotes the concept by means of a trope or metaphor which is peculiar to it; that, consequently, an endless number of nuances, similarities, differences, relationships between objects enter one's consciousness by way of the newly learnt language; that one is therefore given a more complex perception of all things. It follows from this that one thinks differently in every language and also that our thinking is given a new colour and modification each time we learn a new language, that polyglottism is therefore, apart from its many indirect advantages, also what directly educates the mind by correcting and perfecting our views through the emerging complexity and nuancing of concepts; it also heightens our skill in thinking, because the more languages you learn, the more the concept separates itself from the word. The cassical languages do this to a much greater extent than the modern ones, because they differ more from ours; this fact does not allow us to translate word for word, but requires us to melt down our thoughts completely and recast them. (This is one of the many reasons why it is important to learn classical languages.) Or (if I may be allowed a chemical comparison) whereas translation from one modern language into another requires at most that the sentence to be translated should be analysed in its *surface* components and put together again on the basis thereof, translation into Latin very often requires an analysis into its furthest and most basic components (the pure thought content), from which it is then regenerated in totally different forms, so that what is expressed by means of nouns, for instance, in one case is expressed by verbs in the other or *vice versa* — and there are other examples. The same process occurs when one translates from classical into modern languages; this in itself goes to shown how distant an acquaintance with classical authors one is able to make by means of such translations.

Finally, it is easy to see from what has been said that imitation of the style of the ancients in their own languages, which surpass ours by far in grammatical perfection, is the very best way to prepare oneself for the skilful and perfect expression of one's thoughts in one's mother tongue. It is absolutely essential if you want to become a great writer, just as it is necessary for the beginning sculptor or painter to train himself by imitating the examples given by antiquity before he goes on to his own composition. Only by writing in Latin does one learn to treat diction as a work of art whose material is language, which must therefore be treated with the greatest care and caution. It follows that the attention which directs itself at the meaning and value of words, their formation, and their grammatical forms is sharper; you learn how to weigh them precisely and so to handle the precious material which is suited to serving the expression and survival of valuable thoughts; you learn to respect the language you are writing in, so that you do not treat it according to your own whim and · mood, to change its shape. Without this kind of propaedeutics writing easily degenerates into pure hogwash.

A man who knows no Latin is like a man who finds himself in a beautiful landscape in foggy weather; his horizon is extremely limited; he sees clearly only what is close at hand, a few steps beyond that he loses himself in vagueness. The horizon of the man who knows Latin is, on the other hand, very wide;

it encompasses the more recent centuries, the middle ages, antiquity. Greek or even Sanskrit widen the horizon even more of course. Whoever does not know Latin belongs with the *plebs,* even might he be a great virtuoso on the electric machine or have the radical of fluoridic acid in his crucible.

Your writers who do not know Latin will soon be no more to you than swaggering barber's apprentices. They are already well on their way with their gallicisms and would-be light turns of speech. To mediocrity have ye turned, noble Germans, and mediocrity ye shall find. The editions that dare show themselves to the light of day of Greek, indeed even (*horribile dictu!*) of Latin authors with notes in *German* are a true signboard of laziness and a hothouse of ignorance. How is the pupil even to learn Latin if he is constantly interrupted in the tongue his mother speaks. That is why "In schola nil nisi latine" was a good old rule. That the teacher is no longer able to write Latin with ease and the pupil no longer able to read it with ease is the "joke of the matter" (see *Henry V,* Act 2, scene 1) if you please — or if you do not please. Laziness and its daughter ignorance are behind this, nothing else. And it is a shame! The one *hasn't* learnt a thing and the other *doesn't want* to learn a thing. Smoking cigars and dabbling in politics have chased away learning in our time, just as picture books for grown-up children have driven out magazines of literary criticism.

[From Arthur Schopenhauer, *Parerga und Paralipomena* (1815), ch. XXV: "Über Sprache und Worte", § 309, as printed in AS, *Sämmtliche Werke* (ed. Julius Frauenstädt), (Leipzig: Brockhaus, 2. Aufl., 1891). Reprinted in Störig, 101-107.]

Walter Benjamin, 1892-1940

THE CONCEPT OF THE THIRD LANGUAGE

Wherein can the kinship of two languages be found, if we discount historical kinship? Certainly not in the similarity of their words or their literary works. Rather, all suprahistorical kinship of languages rests on the fact that one single thing, the same thing, is intended in each of them as a whole. It can, however, not be reached by any single language but only by the plenitude of their complementary intentions: the pure language. For whereas all simple elements, words, sentences, connections of foreign languages exclude each other, the languages as such complement each other in their very intentions.

The poet's intention is naïve, visual, primary; the translator's secondary, intellectual, derived. For the great motif of the integration of all languages into the one true language fills his work. This is the language in which isolated sentences, literary works, judgments never come to an understanding — which is why they remain at the mercy of translation — but in which languages themselves, complemented and reconciled in the manner of their meaning, agree. And if there is a language of truth, in which the final secrets that all thinking strives to reach are kept, silent and at peace, that language of truth is — the true language.

Rather the meaning of fidelity, which is assured by literalness, is that the great longing for the complementarity of languages should make itself felt in the work. Real translation is transparent, it does not hide the original, it does not steal its light, but allows the pure language, as if reinforced through its own medium, to fall on the original work with greater fulness. This lies above all in the power of literalness in the translation of syntax, and even this points to the word, not the sentence, as the translator's original element.

If that final essence, which is the pure language itself, is, in languages, tied only to the linguistic and its mutations, it is weighed down by heavy and foreign sense in linguistic constructions. To set it free from these, to make the symbolized into the symbolizing itself, to recover the pure language as shaped in linguistic motion, is the immense power given only to translation.

[From Walter Benjamin, "Die Aufgabe des Übersetzers" (1923; foreword to his translation of Baudelaire's *Tableaux parisiens*), as printed in WB, *Schriften* (ed. Th. W. Adorno and Gretel Adorno with Friedrich Podszus), I (Frankfurt/Main: Suhrkamp, 1955). Reprinted in Störig, 156-169. There are various English translations.]

Ulrich von Wilamowitz-Moellendorff, 1848-1931

TRANSLATION, PHILOLOGY, AND CREATIVITY

Only a philologist can translate a Greek poem. Well-intentioned amateurs try
time and again, but if their knowledge of the language is insufficient the results
they achieve are bound to be unsatisfactory as well. Yet translation does not,
therefore, belong to philology. It is above all the result of philological work, but
a result neither planned nor foreseen. The philologist who dutifully strives to
attain a complete understanding of a poem to the best of his ability is com-
pelled against his will to express that understanding, and when he tries to say
what the poet of antiquity has said he tries to do so in his own language: he
translates. That has been my experience. Many of my colleagues share this
experience, and not only in the case of poets of original greatness, but in that of
many texts we explain, as long as they exhibit a fixed style. We the philologists,
dry as dust, who stick to the letter and analyse grammatical subtleties, we also
happen to be perverse enough to love the ideals we serve with all our heart.
Servants we are indeed, but servants of immortal spirits to whom we lend our
mortal mouths: is it surprising that our masters are stronger than we are? Of
course the road is long which leads from such attempts to the completion of a
translation worth its salt. For inspiration of the moment is not enough; it must
be supplemented by the long and thoughtful work of the mind, if something
useful is to be produced. That, then, is no longer philology, no longer our craft.
We cannot do without our philology in this case, but it is not enough. Yet this
should not deter us, in my opinion. Translations of Greek poetry can come into
being only when we, the philologists, make them. And to offer Greek poetry in
such translations to the Germans is only one of the means we need to check the
moral and spiritual decline towards which our nation is moving at increasing
speed; it is probably a weak instrument only, but we philologists are alone in
being able to offer it: we must do our duty as Germans. People do not want to
know too much about us. That is their business, and for many of us the feeling
is mutual. But they also do not want to know anything about the ideals we have
devoted our life to because we believe in them. That cannot leave us indiffer-
ent. Not because of our ideals: they are divine and they have proved that
earthly power does not prevail against them, let alone the wild shouting of the
modern mob of educators. But it is sad to observe how one's own country turns
away from ideals, not just the Greek ideal, but any ideal at all. Gold, sensuality,

honour, those are the gods they believe in; the rest is words. The Greek ideal —
or rather the soul of Greece, which has not died with the bodies of its people,
nor will it ever die — is perfectly capable of turning our people away from this,
not just esthetically and intellectually but morally as well. That is why we need
it. I do not know of much that could perform the same task as well. The real
Goethe, and everything that implies, certainly can, and for many people better;
but to understand him, and I do not mean in the sense of Goethe philologists,
but in such a way that we can accept his wisdom as a beacon for our thoughts
and action, we need the Greek ideal more than ever, because it is presupposed
by that wisdom. What represents the soul of Christianity is certainly also
capable of this, and better for many. But that, too, can co-exist with the Greek
ideal, the more so because that ideal is one of the roots of Christianity itself. But
as long as the churches give our children the stones of the catechism and the
wood of devotional songs instead of the bread of the teachings of Christ, the
result is only too often the killing in man of the inborn striving after that ideal
which tolerates every symbol, but no untruth. Perhaps this will improve when
scholars, those who serve the Greek ideal and those who serve Christianity
alike, will have understood that they belong together because the objects and
the method of their research are the same — or, to put it more correctly, because
they should serve the same master in the same way. It will be clear to some
extent now what I mean when I say that the Greek ideal is indispensable to us
and that it will remain so. If I believe that, how could I fail to recognize my duty
to do what I can to open the way to that ideal? But how? Should I sing its
praises, sell it door to door, should I "popularize science" the way natural
scientists of the common sort do? Far be that from me. Serious people in these
equivalent fields of research obviously think and act the way everybody should
who knows what scholarship is: a matter of work, a pursuit among men in
which only those are able to paticipate who take part in the work. People must
receive the ideal with their own hearts, they must believe in it and live accordingly: to be able to do that they must see for themselves, they must make it
their own. To hear something about it, to satisfy a passing curiosity with it, to
keep a few dead notes in one's memory, these things are of no use. Philology to
the philologists; the Greek ideal, what is immortal in it, to everyone who wants
to come, see, grasp. We must not give the audience a second infusion of our
scholarly work to drink, we must not add to the sour hay of general knowledge
in the cribs of its beloved magazines, we should not conspire with journalists to
put people's thinking in chains by means of ready-made judgments and easy
slogans, as they do. To make the ideal itself accessible to those who are looking
for it, to put it in front of them and always to show them how they should look
at it, what is important: that is, as I see it, what we philologists should do. In so
doing we give our nation the best we have, which is just good enough; and we
give what only those possess who have really understood the Greek nation, its
language, and its nature. That is what we have dedicated our life to and it
cannot be bought for less. But whoever has gathered such possessions should

share them with everyone who wants them. *Noblesse oblige.* It is in this sense that I offer my translations to the public.

This is translation; no more, but also no less. It is not free writing; that we should not be allowed to do, even if we could. But the poet's spirit should come over us and speak with our words. The new lines should have the same effect on their readers as the old ones in their time on their nation and now still on those who have taken the trouble to do the necessary philological work. The requirements are that high. We know very well to how small an extent we meet them; but on earth we can only do what is possible, even though the impossible is required, and we have to know the goal to find the way.

The audience thinks otherwise, of course. Translation must be child's play; children do it, don't they? To lower education standards still more, translation from Greek has taken the place af translation into Greek in our school examinations. Those who have seen samples of these achievements and are able to judge the success of the measure know that too much is required of students on paper, so that they can do too little with impunity. Many an experienced woman teacher and many an inexperienced girl who toil so hard in the honest struggle for bread that it would make a stone weep are given a derisory sum by publishers who argue, "Those are translations; everybody can produce them." They are, of course, often produced accordingly, but the audience is satisfied with them. All you need is a grammar and a lexicon, they think, and those who know the vocabulary or have been given a B in their exam on the language in question can manage without even a grammar.

And if we cannot render a particular expression (in effect we can almost never translate a single word, because two words in two languages never cover each other completely as to the sense, with the exeption of technical terms) we can still, even in German, express a mild reproach which wounds more deeply for that very reason; that is, we can express not just the thought, but also the ethos of a speech. Here, too, it is important to spurn the letter and to follow the spirit, to translate not words or sentences, but to take in thoughts and feelings and to express them. The dress must become new, what is in it must remain. All good translation is travesty. To put it more sharply: the soul remains but it changes bodies; true translation is metempsychosis.

There are, in German, excellent translations from the Greek — so they say. That is an untruth which is repeated with malice or without thinking. It is understandable if enemies of our culture say so, and base on it the argument that there is no need to learn Greek. They achieve their aim that way: nothing is better able to render the originals unattractive than translations. But serious people should be ashamed to hit truth in the face like that.

Goethe cannot be absolved from the reproach that he is mainly responsible for the aberrations and the false glory of German translation. Not through his practice . . . but through his theory. All he demanded of a translation was that it would help his linguistic knowledge – which was very deficient in all languages – to the extent that he would be able to understand the original in its own style. The more the translation was a hybrid, the more it seemed to hold on to the foreign style externally, the better it would perform that task – at least for him. He could see the foreign style through the translation's lack of style, or at least he thought he did. He wanted a mediation of the foreign form; he would mediate the spirit himself. Moreover Goethe was most inclined to acknowledge superior talent wherever he encountered it. He believed what Wilhelm von Humboldt and F[riedrich] A[ugust] Wolf preached to him on the duties of the translator, and he also believed in translations made by his friends.

We don't have to go to great lengths, these days, to state that the metrical theories of these great men are false, consequences of the fateful step Klopstock had taken with his hexameters. Our language and our literature owe very much to this step ... but the attempt to equate quantitative poetry with accented poetry proved possible only because they simply did not understand Greek language and Greek metre. Not Homer, but any porter's way of making Latin verse dressed the *Messias* [Klopstock's epic] in hexameters. In reality language and metre belong together, and it is monstrous to use the German language in conjunction with Greek metre.

It is very remarkable that the Romance languages are almost free from the aberrations of translating in foreign forms. That is because they possess an old culture as well as established styles for their poetry. When Klopstock took the fateful step of wanting to become Virgil and Horace, the Germans had neither a culture nor a well-shaped language, nor even a style, shaped or not. The task was to create them, and imitation was the necessary means to perform it.

It has been done. A number of great men have created our language and our style. They themselves had their doubts as to whether the Germans deserved that gift. Nowadays they would deny it at once, I fear. But deserved or not, the language and the style are there. To translate into German means to translate into the language and the style of our great poets.

This is how matters are: whoever wants to translate a poem must understand it. Once that condition has been met he is faced with the task of recreating what is given in a certain language, with its attendant given metre and style. Innovations can be made in the recreation only to the extent that the original offered something that was new to its language in its time.

[From Ulrich von Wilamowitz-Moellendorff, "Was ist Übersetzen" (1891; foreword to his translation of Euripides' *Hippolytus*), as printed in UvW-M, *Reden und Vorträge*, I (Berlin: Weidmannsche Buchhandlung, 4. Auflage, 1925).]

AGAINST METRICAL TRANSLATION

German classicism tried to transpose the principles of antique metre into German, which led to the belief that all foreign metres could be rendered in our language. It would therefore seem a question of overriding importance whether one can and should translate in Voss's manner or not.

When Klopstock wanted to write an epic poem, the French alexandrine was the form at his disposal, but he was not satisfied with it and he also resented the constraints of rhyme. So he reached out for the Latin hexameter, which writers had already often tried to imitate in German, Gottsched being the latest. The success was enormous; no less so when he went back to the metres of Horace's odes and shaped new stanzas in that vein. That happened also in connection with the writing of neo-Latin poetry, which had been thriving for centuries. He did not even think of Greek. But now Homer had been discovered, so to speak: people wanted him in German and Fritz Stolberg forced his *Iliad* in hexameters upon them; [Gottfried August] Bürger still preferred blank verse. One still wrote without much insight into the rules of antiquity, one was not too conversant with the language and no one knew the first rudiments of Greek metre. Enter Voss, who had enjoyed a better training in philology, and was the first consciously to impose a quantitative metre upon the Germans, the more rigorously so the older he got. Countless attempts followed. Goethe dared the ultimate in the *Pandora*, with its Ionic metre. Platen invented new metres in Pindar's style, and had to print their diagrams before the poems, as was the custom in the Greek editions of Pindar. Nor did things stop here: Firdausı's Persian verse and the epic metre of the Indians were recreated, even though they simply cannot be spoken in German, and neither can the Ionic metre. Nor can it be ignored that the German example influenced other Germanic languages, and even though this did not lead to great, generally recognized poetry in antique metres, translations have often been attempted in this vein. The French must make do with prose; the Italians may attempt more, even against the nature of their beautiful language.

Everyone should know by now that this whole direction is wrong, that it goes against the very nature of language, because the Germanic languages, or rather all contemporary European languages, do not have long and short but stressed and unstressed syllables. Poets have, in fact, abandoned that direction by now, and only the hexameter and the distichon and perhaps a couple of metres taken from odes are still used occasionally, though not a single one has become popular.

But how should we render the poetry of antiquity? One thing must be stated first: Homer is untranslatable because we do not have an epic metre, because we do not write stories in verse. Any somehow stanzaic metre disrupts the free movement of the Homeric story, and a pair of rhymes already amounts to a distichon. But the style, too, is inimitable because it is, in many respects, formulaic and because of its ornamental words: Homer is not popular poetry, but definitely the poetry of high art. A Homer in prose must divest himself of his jewels, in other words lose all the colour of life. The outlook is better for the dialogue of the drama, because in this case we have our classical style and a verse form wich can be modified to suit comedy too, even though we have yet to find an artist to do this for Menander. For the epigram one could take Goethe's distichs (rarely, I believe), but they are no use for the Greek elegy, nor for Propertius, for instance, because they are Ovidic. And no rules can be given for all poetry wich was sung, for all lyrical poetry, and for the Hellenistic and Roman poetry of high art. Whoever wants to try them should, in any case, look for a German form analogous to the original in mood and style; let him decide to what extent he can adapt himself to the form of the original. What his intention is, as a translator, will be a decisive factor, and so, too, will be his understanding of the text. It is very informative, in this respect, to look at Stolberg's *Iliad* or Wieland's Shakespeare. Their understanding is severely limited, but their rendering is adequate, as far as it goes. One could imagine that someone would be attracted by the general impression of nobility, splendour, and strange sonority in Pindar, and the result might be something which is formally impressive, even though it renders nothing at all of Pindar's individual art, because the translator decided to stick to the surface, to what is conventional. It must be required that he should have a feeling for the foreign language in its finest nuances and that he should come so close to the poet that he can register the motions of the poet's soul in his own. Whether he has, in addition to this, the artistic ability to render this understanding in the translation is a different matter altogether. But even when he remains imperfect he will still achieve what Goethe praises in Wieland's translations in his address on Wieland: he will share insight with us, that we may share his pleasure. He would merely be putting obstacles in his own path if he were to engage in the vain endeavour of trying to keep to the metres of the original, as Voss, and better men than Voss, Humboldt, for instance, attempted to do. Their translations are completely dead now, as is Schleiermacher's Plato. The matter is totally different when a creative poet takes up an ancient work and recreatively transforms it in his own spirit. This is something quite legitimate, even greater, but it is not a translation. For translation only wants to let the ancient poet speak to us clearly, and in a manner as immediately intelligible, as he spoke in his own time. He must be given words, he must speak through our mouth. "True translation is metempsychosis." This implies that the ancient poet, whose own lines lead an immortal life, must time and again cast his spirit on a new translator, because translations are mortal, indeed even shortlived. And if an old philologist who has often tried his hand at it is to say how it should be done, he can indicate how it should not be done, but for the rest he will know better than to give recipes. Necessary though it is, learning is not sufficient, not even to understand the text, and when translation is also something like the writing of poetry, the help of the Muse is most certainly needed.

[From Ulrich von Wilamowitz-Moellendorff, "Die Kunst der Übersetzung", in *Der Spiegel* (Jahrbuch des Propyläen Verlages; 1924), 21-25. Reprinted in Störig, 139-143.]

Rudolf Borchardt, 1877-1945

TRANSLATION AS AN ACT OF RESTORATION

There came, at last, historically speaking, the final disintegration of Romanticism, the time of pink roses, during which one could do everything, when all was easy and in which there were still problems left, but no one to feel them, where the levity of merciless bourgeois philistinism which seems to us today almost mystical, in its benevolent barbaric immaturity . . . [led to a] bankruptcy of language and styles.

The circle of the historical exchange of forms between nations closes in that Germany returns to the foreign object what it has learnt from it and freely improved upon. It pays for its cultural debts in the same currency in which it made them and in doing so it grows richer, according to the old merchant proverb "who pays his debts betters his fortune". That this new wealth is immediately followed by the recklessness of the *nouveau riche* is not surprising. That the conquered form, abstracted from the conditions under which it was possessed, was immediately overworked and spread thin in totally heterogeneous ventures only goes to prove the old German energy with which the nation tries, consciously or unconsciously, youthful, immature, self-assured and resolved to every sarifice, to make good at one stroke the cultural neglect of centuries.

[From Rudolf Borchardt, "Dante und deutscher Dante" (1908), as printed in RB, *Gesammelte Werke in Einzelbänden, Prosa*, II (Stuttgart: Klett, 1959). Partially reprinted in Störig, 144-155.]

Franz Rosenzweig, 1886-1929

To translate means to serve two masters. Which is why nobody can do it. Which is why it is, in practice, everybody's task, like all the other things nobody is able to do in theory. Everybody has to translate and everybody does. Whoever speaks translates from his opinion into the presupposed understanding of another, and not the understanding of a non-existent general "other" either, but of this very concrete other he sees in front of him and whose eyes light up or fall shut, depending on how he translates. Whoever hears, translates words that sound in his ears into his intellect, that is, practically speaking, into the language of his mouth. Everybody has his own language. Or rather: everybody would have his own language if there really was such a thing as monological speech (as the logicians, those would-be monologicians, claim) and if all speech was not, in reality, dialogue.

If all speech is translation, that theoretical impossibility of translation we recognize and acknowledge can only have the kind of meaning for us which all such theoretical impossibilities, acknowledged from the stork's perspective of those who stand before life, acquire in life later on: it will give us the courage of modesty in the "impossible" and necessary compromises, the succession of which is called life, the courage automatically required, not by the impossible we acknowledge, but by the necessary we give up. For speaking and listening this implies not that the other should have my mouth or my ears, which would obviously render translation superfluous, but speaking and listening as well. And in the speaking and listening between nations this implies not that the translation — is not translation, but either the original, which would render the nation which listens superfluous, or a new original, which would be the end of the nation which speaks. Only a mad egoism under the delusion that it could satisfy its every need in its own individual or national existence, and wishing to be surrounded by a desert, could possibly want either. In a world which has not been created to be a desert, but in divisions and according to species, there is no room for such an attitude.

Schleiermacher, himself among the great translators with his Plato, once wittily enough disinguished between translations which leave the writer in peace as much as possible and move the reader towards him and those which leave the reader in peace as much as possible and move the writer towards him. We know now, after what has been said before, that this sparkling antithesis, in so far as it really aspired to remain an antithesis, was really not much more than sparkling. For if it aspired to be more than the antithetically clarifying illumination of a very complex and entangled and never antithetically separated reality, the ideal of a Plato translation would be either a textual edition in the Teubner series or Kant's *Critique of Pure Reason*. But taken with common sense, in other words not as an either/or but as a means to disentangle a tangled reality, those words of Schleiermacher's can lead us into our research and keep us company for part of the way. They can teach us to raise the question as to the proportion of the mixture; and when this question – which is, like all quantitative questions, very important but, again like all quantitative questions, only preliminary in nature – has found its answer, it can lead us to the real question: at which points in the work is the reader moved and at which points the original? As always the mere naming of the operative forces says nothing at all here: the establishment of their quantitative relationship says something, but little; only the description of the points where one starts and where the other will give us an image.

[From Franz Rosenzweig, *Die Schrift und Luther* (1926), as printed in Martin Buber and FR, *Die Schrift und ihre Verdeutschung* (Berlin: Schocken, 1936), 88-129. Reprinted in Störig, 194-222.]

References

THE TRADITION

For bibliographical information on the texts and passages given in this book in translation, see the end notes following each text. The only extensive collection of writings in German of the kind presented here is:

Störig, Hans Joachim (ed.), 1963. *Das Problem des Übersetzens.* Wege der Forschung, 8. Darmstadt: Wissenschaftliche Buchgesellschaft. (2. veränderte Aufl., 1969; 3. Aufl., with an "Ausgewähltes Schrifttum" [Select Bibliography], 1973.)

Störig's volume brings together writings by various of the authors included above (Luther, Novalis, Goethe, Schleiermacher, von Humboldt, A. W. Schlegel, Schopenhauer, Grimm, von Wilamowitz-Moellendorff, Borchardt, Benjamin, Vossler, and Rosenzweig), though the selection is not always the same. Also included in Störig are several other nineteenth- and twentieth-century writers in German (Friedrich Nietzsche, Wolfgang Schadewaldt, Eduard Horst von Tscharner, Ludwig W. Kahn, Martin Buber, Martin Heidegger, Peter Brang, Hans-Georg Gadamer, and Karl Dedecius), as well as a few translated from other languages (Jerome, José Ortega y Gasset, Edmond Cary, and Anthony G. Oettinger).

ON THE TRADITION

The four major studies of the German tradition are the following:

Huber, Thomas, 1968. *Studien zur Theorie des Übersetzens im Zeitalter der deutschen Aufklärung 1730-1770.* Deutsche Studien, 7. Mannheim am Glan: Hain.

Huyssen, Andreas, 1969. *Die frühromantische Konzeption von Übersetzung und Aneignung. Studien zur frühromantischen Utopie einer deutschen Weltliteratur.* Zürcher Beiträge zur deutschen Literatur- und Geistesgeschichte, 33. Zürich: Atlantis.

Sdun, Winfried, 1967. *Probleme und Theorien des Übersetzens in Deutschland vom 18. bis zum 20. Jahrhundert.* München: Hueber.

Senger, Anneliese, 1971. *Deutsche Übersetzungstheorie im 18. Jahrhundert.* Abhandlungen zur Kunst-, Musik- und Literaturwissenschaft, 97. Bonn: Bouvier.

A more summary survey is provided by an older frequently cited study:

Fränzel, Walter, 1914. *Geschichte des Übersetzens im 18. Jahrhundert.* Beiträge zur Kultur- und Universalgeschichte, 25. Leipzig: Voigtländer.

Parts of the two following more general studies are also useful:

Kloepfer, Rolf, 1967. *Die Theorie der literarischen Übersetzung. Romanisch-deutscher Sprachbereich.* Freiburger Schriften zur romanischen Philologie, 12. München: Fink.

Wuthenow, Ralph-Rainer, 1969. *Das fremde Kunstwerk. Aspekte der literarischen Übersetzung.* Palaestra, 252. Göttingen: Vandenhoeck & Ruprecht. (See esp. ch. II: "Geschichte und Theorie", pp. 29-71.)

OTHER

Radnitzky. Gerard. 1970. *Contemporary Schools of Metascience.* 2nd rev. & enlarged ed., Göteborg: Universitetsfor-
    laget. (1st. ed. Göteborg: Akademiforlaget. 1968; 3rd enl. ed., Chicago: Regnery. 1973.)
Seifert. Helmut. 1973. *Einführung in die Wissenschaftstheorie.* II. Beck'sche Schwarze Reihe. 5. unveränderte Aufl.,
    München: Beck. (1. Aufl., München: Beck. 1970.)

Index of Names

Printed in the United States
By Bookmasters